HOW TO BE DEPRESSED: A GUIDE

BY DANA EAGLE

KNOCK KNOCK®

VENICE, CALIFORNIA

Created, published, and distributed by Knock Knock
1635-B Electric Ave.
Venice, CA 90291
knockknockstuff.com
Knock Knock is a registered trademark of Knock Knock LLC

This book is a work of editorial nonfiction meant solely for entertainment purposes. It is not intended to advocate any particular course of action in any situation. It is also not intended to diagnose or treat any psychiatric, psychological, emotional, or physical problem. Following the directives indicated in this book would not only be tragically literal, it could also be illegal, immoral, or downright dangerous. In no event will Knock Knock be liable to any reader for any damages, including direct, indirect, incidental, special, consequential, or punitive damages, arising out of or in connection with the use of the information contained in this book. So there.

Where specific company, product, and brand names are cited, copyright and trademarks associated with these names are property of their respective owners.

ISBN: 978-160106917-7
UPC: 825703-50231-2

10 9 8 7 6 5 4 3 2 1

80% OF THE POPULATION
SUFFERS FROM DEPRESSION.
THE OTHER 20% CAUSE IT.

—DANA EAGLE

TABLE OF CONTENTS

INTRODUCTION: WELCOME TO DEPRESSION   9

➢ We've Been Waiting for You   9

➢ Take the Quiz: Do You Have What It Takes to Be Depressed?   11

➢ Sources of Depression   12

CHAPTER 1: GETTING STARTED   13

➢ Stocking Up   15

➢ What You Will Need / What You Will Not Need   16

➢ The Depression Code of Honor   17

➢ Responding to the Question "What's Wrong?"   18

➢ Guided Body Meditation   19

➢ Who to Contact   20

➢ For the Political Depressive   22

➢ Psychiatric Evaluation: The Desperation Proclamation   23

➢ Taking Your Depressed Thinking to the Next Level   24

➢ Depressed Fashions   26

➢ Types of Depressives   28

➢ Where to Be Depressed   30

➢ My Depression Was Born On   32

➢ FAQ   33

➢ Depression Milestones   34

➢ Getting Started Wrap-Up   38

CHAPTER 2: BUILDING YOUR DEPRESSION FOUNDATION 39

➢ Regret: Learning to Live in the Past 40

➢ Family Regret 41

➢ The Precious Moments of Regret 42

➢ The Human Life Cycle of Regret 44

➢ Time's Up! (Regret Boosters) 46

➢ Find Your Depression Match 47

➢ Anxiety: Fear the Future! 50

➢ Anxiety Boosts 52

➢ Medley of Despair: Word-Find Game 54

➢ Goodnight Gloom: A Worrier's Bedtime Story 57

➢ Depression Foundation Wrap-Up 58

CHAPTER 3: IT'S A SAD, SAD, SAD, SAD WORLD 59

➢ Thoughts & Feelings 60

➢ Thought-Evaluation System 61

➢ Daily Negations 62

➢ Finding Your Depressed Pose 64

➢ How to Leave Things Unfinished 66

➢ Depression on a Budget 68

➢ Psychiatric Evaluation: Good Grief 70

➢ Depression Travel Guide 71

➢ I Ruined It 79

➢ Sad, Sad World Wrap-Up 82

CHAPTER 4: YOU ARE NOT ALONE (BUT YOU *ARE* LONELY) 83

- ➤ Happy People Are Ruining Our Lives   84
- ➤ Happiness for Sale   86
- ➤ Urban Myths   88
- ➤ Building Your Depressed Community   90
- ➤ Depressed-Friend Guestbook   92
- ➤ Depressed-Friend Activities   94
- ➤ Make Your Own!   96
- ➤ Not Alone But Lonely Wrap-Up   98

CHAPTER 5: TREATMENT (HOW TO MAKE IT NOT WORK FOR YOU) 99

- ➤ Where to Turn: Therapist, Psychic, Dog?   100
- ➤ Psychologist, Analyst, or Socialist?   102
- ➤ Buyer Beware: State License or Monogram?   103
- ➤ Lesser-Known Therapies   104
- ➤ Types of Therapists   106
- ➤ Side-Effects Word Scramble   108
- ➤ Psychiatric Evaluation: A Doom of Her Own   109
- ➤ Things You Shouldn't Say to Your Therapist   110
- ➤ Things You Hope Your Therapist Doesn't Say to You   111
- ➤ Treatment Wrap-Up   112

CHAPTER 6: FUN WITH DEPRESSION!   113

> Finding Your Depression Alias   114

> 13 Books to Cheer You Up!   116

> Depressing Pets   117

> Depression Inaction Figures: Collect the Whole Set!   123

> 13 Flicks to Cheer You Up!   128

> What's Wrong with Me? Moody Catcher   129

> Fun Depressing Foods   131

> Depression Horrorscopes   132

> Your Bad Poetry   136

> 13 Songs to Cheer You Up!   138

> 4PM Options   139

> Fun with Depression Wrap-Up   140

DEPRESSION EPILOGUE   142

ACKNOWLEDGMENTS   144

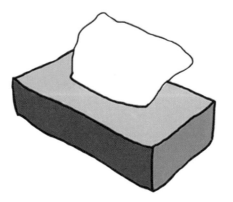

WE'VE BEEN WAITING FOR YOU

Welcome to depression! Perhaps you arrived here by way of a bad relationship, a childhood trauma, a near-death experience, a feels-like-a-death experience, or an Adele concert. Or perhaps, more likely, you're not sure how you got here at all.

It may be surprising to learn that many people don't believe depression exists. Rather, they view it as a human construct, like capitalism, communications majors, or God.

The fact is much of what we know about depression is made up. I'm making stuff up right now. It's what scientists refer to as "anecdotal evidence," a record of just a handful of people's experiences. Or, in the case of depression, the misery and despair of billions.

But without a definite cause (or way to measure tears), it's impossible to prove depression's existence. And thus it would be impractical, even downright irresponsible, to invest in a cure. After all, we don't even know if the tears are man-made or environmental. Do you understand the negative impact a cure could have on the economy and jobs? Without depression in the world, doctors, clergymen, and psychics would be out of work—not to mention fortune cookies, wishing fountains, tattoo parlors, and bars.

Still you may be asking, "But why would I want to be depressed?" Well, guess what? You already are.

Oh, did you think this was just a slump? A bad week or decade? Many who drop in do. In fact, it's not unusual for one to have to be informed they are depressed. That's because depression can appear quite subtly. Like toilet paper on your shoe, you don't always see it until someone else points it out.

Yup, depression is sneaky. It has many potential routes in. It can be the outcome of a traumatic event, like birth, or a *truly* traumatic event, like your sister's birth. While it might begin as the temporary by-product of a life-altering catastrophe, it maintains an ability to survive—even thrive—long after the original trauma fades.

This guide is your chance to start right from where you are—blue, dep-curious, or ninety miles past the nuthouse. It's a playbook for your time on the bench. So whether you're here deliberately, or you've been invited by a friend or uncovered by an NPR mailing list, there's a great deal of fun to be had.

Finally, a note to the happy: Have you noticed your numbers dwindling? Of course not. You're too busy whistling, which for the record is only fun for the whistler. Many of your kind have defected here. You see, no one gets through life unscathed.

But this book isn't just for the clinically depressed or those who want to be. It's for people who grasp the inevitability of life's speed bumps, the unfortunate losses, like divorce, death, and spotty wi-fi signals. It's for those who've had dark flashes and wondered, Huh? What was that?

But you, happy person, you're not depressed. So why should you read this book? Look, it's only fair. After all, we've read all of yours.

TAKE THE QUIZ:

DO YOU HAVE WHAT IT TAKES TO BE DEPRESSED?

	Yes	No
Did you have a bad childhood? (Hint: Did you have parents?)	10	1
When you hear other people say they are happy, do you think they just have really low standards?	10	1
Do you write poetry?	10	1
Does your poetry have tear stains on it?	10	1
When your mom says she's proud, do you sense she's holding back laughter?	10	1
Do you have more than one doctor on speed dial?	10	1
Have you ever wished you could hold your feelings in your hands and shove them into other people's chests just for a second so they can feel what you're feeling?	10	1
Do you think your life would significantly improve if you were in prison?	10	1
Do you go to bed early, not necessarily because you're tired but because you don't want to be awake anymore?	10	1
Will you likely not get around to adding up these points?	10	1

If you scored between 1 and 100 (or skipped to the bottom to read this), congratulations! You have what it takes to be depressed.

SOURCES OF DEPRESSION

1. SELF-ABSORPTION
2. ALCOHOL
3. DAIRY
4. PROCRASTINATION
5. LIST MAKING

CHAPTER 1

GETTING STARTED

First, you're going to need sweatpants. You'll need only one pair. Any more can disrupt the process. I recommend the flannel-pajama-pants hybrid. The kind that could be pants, could be long underwear—who knows? They are cries for help that ensure no one will want to help.

In all likelihood, you won't be leaving home anytime soon, but there is no need to concern yourself with provisions. The key to executing a successful depression plan is not having one at all.

PLEASE SIGN IN HERE:

HERE IS A MAP OF LOCAL SCENES AND ATTRACTIONS (VERY LOCAL)

STOCKING UP

You will need a sofa, but a floor will do. Get an afghan. This will serve as blanket, towel, napkin, tissue, and bib. Should you decide to engage in the precarious act of walking, wrap the afghan around your head. This is womb, shell, shield, and prep for when you go homeless. Move slowly, or not at all. Your body has the muscle strength of a baby carp—it may smell like one too. It can flop from place to place. It cannot pick up the mail. It can pick up the remote.

Meanwhile, your mind is trying to escape a familiar pain known as consciousness. You may stare, sleep, cry, or all of the above. You may be able to watch TV, but you may not be able to retain any information. If you are foolhardy enough to read, forget books (other than this one). Stick with headlines, refrigerator magnets, and closed captioning.

Additional activities include forgetting what you're supposed to be doing, avoiding others, consuming the contents of your earthquake-preparedness kit, exploring the space between the sofa and the wall, timing exactly how long it takes for your foot to fall asleep, and counting the number of times the news anchor says, "We'll be back!" (to which you reply in a creepy voice, "I'll be waiting."). Ultimately, your job is to isolate and exist—not necessarily in that order.

The following chapter will guide you through gathering the emotions, excuses, and gear you will need for the journey of not going anywhere. The good news is that whether you've packed appropriately for the trip or not really won't make much of a difference. Nothing will! Nothing ever does. Is it nap time already?

WHAT YOU WILL NEED	WHAT YOU WILL NOT NEED
Cake	Parties
NPR	Fresh air
Mood swings	Mood lighting
Parking tickets	Concert tickets
Physicians' Desk Reference	*Martial Arts Instructor's Desk Reference*
Anything stained (including reputation)	Laundry detergent
Nature videos where large creatures eat adorable, helpless ones	Nature
Indecision	Charisma
Second-guessing	Determination
Indecision or second-guessing	Charm
Streaming episodes of *Friends*	Actual friends
Motive	Motivation
Playing cards	Business cards
Time magazine's "30 Under 30"	*People* magazine's "What Went Wrong"
Happy people saying, "You have to have a sense of humor about things."	Happy people

THE DEPRESSION CODE OF HONOR

Please raise your right hand. The one with the tissue in it.

I, [state your name] do solemnly swear to the Depression Code of Honor:

To be so wrapped up in my own problems that I have neither the will, ability, nor awareness to consider those around me.

And, regardless of human tragedy, disaster, or unjust awards shows, I shall steadfastly remain convinced that no one has it worse than me and shall act accordingly.

Declared on the _____ day of _____, 20 _____.

RESPONDING TO THE QUESTION "WHAT'S WRONG?"

There are so many things that can be wrong with you, but when someone asks, "What's wrong?" there are really only two ways to answer this question. You must sigh loudly and state unconvincingly, "Nothing." It's either that, or go all in. Don't stop. Blurt out everything: your fears, your resentments, that time your mother dressed you in red, white, and blue for the Statue of Liberty class trip.

Consider any exchange boundless consent. Call them in the middle of the night or at work and say, "I'm not bothering you, right? You said to call anytime..."

When you sense that someone's on the verge of telling you off, verbally berate yourself before they have the chance to: "I'm such a jerk. No wonder I have no friends. I'm just so lonely. You're my only true friend." Tell them what a fragile time your therapist said this was for you. If they try to tell you about their day, life, or problems, use each one as a jumping-off point for something else you just had to tell them. Should they find an entry point for themselves in the conversation, tell them that you're ready to get off the phone. Unless, of course, you can lure them over. We do accept recruits.

NOTHING.

GUIDED BODY MEDITATION

Scientists have discovered a mind-body connection: people with great bodies don't care about their minds. The following meditation is an exercise for people who can't be bothered to exercise.

> ➤ Begin by closing your eyes. Don't relax. Feel the weight of your body, the weight of your head. Wow, that thing is heavy!

> ➤ Imagine yourself going down a river. Stay focused, or you'll drown.

> ➤ Feel yourself bobbing gently in the current. The water probably has some flesh-eating bacteria, so keep your mouth closed.

> ➤ As you float down the river, feel at one with decay.

> ➤ You hit your head on a rock. Yeah, painful.

> ➤ Breathe. It's only a tiny bit of blood.

> ➤ You arrive at a clearing. Step out of the water and into a meadow.

> ➤ Open your mind's eye. What do you see? Flowers? Butterflies? How 'bout ticks? You have to check for ticks. Lyme disease is a serious disorder that no doctor ever believes you have because it is nearly impossible to diagnose before your nerves shut down and you die.

> ➤ Now just allow yourself to relax and think about death.

> ➤ Okay, now open your eyes. Bring yourself back to your surroundings.

> ➤ How do you feel? Embarrassed? Yeah, that was weird.

WHO TO CONTACT

Let's be clear: it is not necessary to make contact with the outside world. However, if you have the energy and are in need of additional pointless activities, the following list of contacts will reinforce disconnection, loneliness, and help fortify the fortress of isolation.

LOCAL THERAPISTS
Call local therapists to find out if they offer sliding-scale fees for people who've already slid. When you find a therapist you like, tell her you'd like to know more about purchasing the extended warranty.

YOUR CABLE COMPANY
Inform the representative you are going to need more channels and will be home for the appointment scheduled between 8AM and End Times. If they are able to make the change over the phone, tell them you'll be waiting anyway.

MAIL-ORDER PHARMACEUTICALS
Request a detailed catalog of every available pill and a description of what it fixes. Find out if the person helping you has any favorites, and ask which goes better with chicken.

YOUR EX
Text your ex to tell him you just realized you are not thinking of him, though just for fun, you'd like to renew the breakup because the fighting was always more satisfying than the lovemaking.

**YOUR HEALTH
INSURANCE COMPANY**
Contact customer service to
review your Explanation of
Benefits. Tell the representative you don't feel like this is an
Explanation of Benefits, but
rather an Explanation of Withholding Benefits. Follow that up
by requesting an Explanation of
Someone Else's Better Benefits.

A HACKER
Offer a hacker the opportunity
to steal your identity, but only
if they'll offer someone else's
life in exchange. Maybe be cagey
about your life details.

HOSPITALS
Tell them you're looking for a
quick getaway to re-energize you.
Ask if they offer AAA discounts,
turndown service, brunch, and
free wi-fi.

A FORMER THERAPIST
Call your old therapist, and let
her know how you're doing. Ask
her if those Jungian archetypes
work this well for everyone.

A PONY
Reflect on the years devoted to
therapy, and consider a pony.
Also useless and expensive but
more fun to comb.

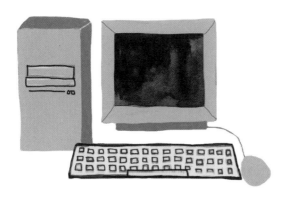

FOR THE POLITICAL DEPRESSIVE

If you'd like to compound despair, politics is for you! It virtually guarantees that even after a long and exhausting debate, nothing will change. Reach out to the following government agencies, and discover a system more broken than your dreams.

SENATE HEARING COMMITTEE

Write the Senate Hearing Committee and tell them you are not feeling heard.

EDWARD SNOWDEN, DANIEL ELLSBERG, CHELSEA MANNING, WIKILEAKS, JULIAN ASSANGE

Notify the nation's leading informants that you have uncovered lies and secrets no one cares about either.

NSA

Call the NSA and convey your gratitude: "Thanks for listening. I'm glad someone is." (Then again, they're probably listening right now. You could just say it out loud.)

STATE ELECTION BOARD

Inform your election board you plan a bid for office. Run a smear campaign against yourself: "I can't help you. I can't even help me. But with your vote, I can win a seat in Congress—and I am really good at sitting! As your candidate, I pledge to do nothing other than accept the free lifetime health benefits awarded to each Representative." (Paid for by Sitizens for Sitting).

UNITED NATIONS DIPLOMAT

Contact a diplomat from a war-torn country, and commiserate on the elusiveness of the peace process.

PSYCHIATRIC EVALUATION:
The Desperation Proclamation

PATIENT INFORMATION
Patient Name: Abraham Lincoln

Lived: February 12, 1809-April 15, 1865

Employment: Farmer. Lawyer. Commander in Chief. Hypochondriac.

CASE HISTORY
Symptoms:

Depression. Patient describes it like a bullet to the head.

Childhood:

- Born in a log cabin with no syrup, his parents were members of the Baptist Church but broke away due to their opposition to slavery and waking up early on Sundays.
- As a child, Lincoln was kicked in the head by a mule that later caused seizures and his decision to be a republican.

Physical Issues:

Oddly tall yet insists on a stovepipe hat. maybe that's where he hid the logs?

Risk Factors:
- Withholding father
- Dead mother (described as very withholding)
- Death of sister
- Assassination threats
- Copperheads
- Alcoholic generals
- Slave-owning in-laws (makes for awkward holidays)
- Death of favorite child (and having it revealed to his other children that he had a favorite child)

Assessment:

In this case, it's not that patient had depression. It's more like depression had him. If he'd been happy, something would've been wrong.

Recommended Treatment:
- Add splash of color to the wardrobe
- Keep the top hat but spring for a cane, jazz shoes, and take the missus out for some ballroom dance.
- Learn a card trick. Pour water in the hat, and Abracadabra! You've made slavery disappear! And what's that up your sleeve? The national banking system.

TAKING YOUR DEPRESSED THINKING TO THE NEXT LEVEL

There's no point in doing depression halfway. After all, it's the only thing you'll be doing well for the next several months. If you want to go from merely bummed out to full-on depression, you're going to have to get your mind in the game.

Let's begin: Right now you have problems. Lots of them. Conflicts, stressful situations, and demands you can't meet—standard, universal stuff. There is one issue, however, that's more troubling than the others. That's the one! Let's work with it.

Before you consider your issue and the impact it may have on your life, you need to consider what other people think of you. In particular, focus on those you feel at odds with. Whether they know about your current conflict or not is completely irrelevant. Accept that they are keeping tabs, but only on your errors. Some may say, "You are not a mind reader!" No, but you are a *tension feeler*. Remember, this is not about their divorce, their impending layoff, or whatever their thing is. It is about the fact that their unusually brief greeting at the water cooler means they are definitely judging you.

You're now close to leveling up. To make that final leap, here are a few final points. Practice these diligently, and you'll be a level-two loser before you know it.

DEPRESSION TIP #1:
DISREGARD BENEFIT OF THE DOUBT
It will never benefit you. Consider the best and the worst possible outcomes. Now eliminate the best. From now on, there is no gray area. Your circumstances are either awful or amazing. Hint: they are not amazing.

DEPRESSION TIP #2:
ACCEPT FEELINGS ARE FACTS
If you feel bad, it is bad. Yes, you have a looming disaster on your hands. But don't get cocky. You're still at level one. For level two, simply take it up a notch. Look at the remaining areas of your life, whether health, love, work, family, or money. Have a mixer and introduce your problems to each other! See how much they have in common: you.

DEPRESSION TIP #3:
LEARN FROM THE PAST THAT YOU DO NOT LEARN
In the middle of all those whirling thoughts, don't forget to fixate on general themes like:

> People forget me.

> I'm incompitent. (Make sure to spell it wrong.)

> Something went wrong a long time ago.

DEPRESSED

UNSHAVEN
You believe your unshaven face conveys "hipster," but those uneven patches say "Unabomber."

BASEBALL CAP
Been on your head so long you forgot which team you're supporting — or bringing down.

MORRISSEY SHIRT
Because 1991 reminds you you're 40.

HYGIENE FOR THE DEPRESSED

INSTEAD OF:	TRY:
Toothpaste	Mouthwas
Soap	Purell
Clean socks	Dirty Socks
Clean underwear	Inside-out underwear

FLANNEL PANTS
Who needs a date? You've got porn.

FLIP-FLOPS
You can never find them when you need them because they're trying to escape your life.

BLACK DRESS SOCKS
Proof to others you once had a job. Proof to yourself you're becoming your dad.

FASHIONS

LOOSE FITTING UNIVERSITY SWEATSHIRT

Disguises the fact that you are not wearing a bra. And gives you the cover of hardworking student studying for finals. Beneath is an...

UNCOMFORTABLY TIGHT FITTING HELLO KITTY TEE

To remind you to stop eating. You'll learn to ignore it.

HAIR SCRUNCHY

At this point more hair is stuck to it than to your head.

VASELINE

Instead of lip gloss.

HELLO KITTY

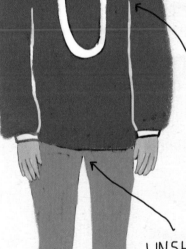

YOGA PANTS
(AKA LOUNGEWEAR)

Code for "Slept in."

UNSHAVEN

Forget about cutting. The stubble alone makes you a danger to yourself.

TYPES OF DEPRESSIVES

What kind of depressive are you? Professional depressives don't announce they are depressed. They select an overarching theme to mask the struggle. Here are some classic depressive archetypes to choose from—or just freestyle and invent your own!

"I'M FINE" DEPRESSIVE
Not a hair out of place and always where she's supposed to be. In Hell. She can't slow down because she's late for pilates, and if she misses class her core will explode, and then who is going to cover carpool?

PROJECTOR DEPRESSIVE
The Projector asks, "How are you? No, really. You sure you're alright?" She asks suspiciously, second-guessing your answer but never her own motivation, which is to deflect her own torment. Also known as a therapist.

DUMPED DEPRESSIVE
Has one relationship he never got past. Usually, it's with his mother. She's seeing other depressives now.

TEXTING DEPRESSIVE
"Things are 🙁. Bit of a 👎 day.... Hello? Sometimes I feel like you're not even reading these. 😭 😭 😭 "

"BREAKTHROUGH" DEPRESSIVE
Every six months or so the "Breakthrough" Depressive discovers "it"—a transforming experience, religion, or book that offers the key to total happiness. This time he really "got it" though. You can, too, by making five easy installments of $19.99.

SOBER DEPRESSIVE
She's sober now. Still depressed, but sober! Did she tell you that she's sober?

IRRATIONAL-FITS-OF-ANGER DEPRESSIVE

Hard to say if she is depressed or using her residual free-floating anger as an excuse for keying your car.

RETAIL DEPRESSIVE

Consistently appears with new big-ticket items: "Well, I just had to treat myself. I couldn't drive around in that beat-up thing. It wasn't good for my soul." Apparently, bankruptcy is.

CICADA DEPRESSIVE

Emerges every five to seven years. When you ask, "Where've you been?" He simply says, "I just had to work some stuff out."

BREAKING-BAD-NEWS DEPRESSIVE

Something awful is happening somewhere, and Breaking-Bad-News Depressive will keep you on high alert. Board up your home! It could be a vicious storm, a rare tropical bird flu, or worse—the BBND himself.

CHRONIC-SOMETHING DEPRESSIVE

She will never admit depression is the main source of her difficulty. Rather, she suffers from "real" illnesses, like exhaustion, food allergies, or hypochondria.

POT SMOKIN' DEPRESSIVE

Totally not depressed. Just chillin' out. Believes pot is not a drug—it's just a natural thing, sourced from the earth, like coal. He'll contend that this plant has been embraced by healers, musicians, and countless of the unemployed.

ANIMAL RIGHTS DEPRESSIVE

She is doing fine. She just feels sad for her animal, *your* animal, *all* animals. You can't possibly understand how vital these creatures are. Not only do they love her unconditionally, but they lack the ability to tell her to shut up.

WHERE TO BE DEPRESSED

Every so often, the depressed must return to the world to remember why they left. Such excursions can bring to life the apathy you feel toward others. Below are locales that will serve as reminders of the darkness that awaits outside the safety of your bed covers.

THE BOOKSTORE
Seek out literature, poems, and overpromising "secrets" of success. While you're there, return your most recent self-help purchase. When asked for a reason, say with stone-faced determination, "Look at me. Do I look like I've awakened the giant within?"

THE DMV
Renewing your driver's license allows you to come in contact with officials willing to accept whatever weight you tell them. Bathing and combing your hair are optional because DMV cameras have a magic lens that makes everyone look sad and guilty. When asked if you'd like to be an organ donor say, "Yes, and I'd like to get started right now."

THE PET-RESCUE CENTER
Ask the volunteer on duty what the policy on "people rescue" is, and let him know you're available for adoption, house-trained, and willing to be euthanized.

COFFEE SHOPS

Coffee shops are the best. Here is a place where, as much as you try to wallow in your own self-absorption, someone will want to speak with you about their own depression—a kind of Depression Smack Down. People look at you and see a face that says, "Come, sit down, tell me about your screenplay, conspiracy theories, and communications with the dead."

THE PHARMACY

You'll likely find some kindred depressed spirits at the pharmacy— people who are at death's door and looking forward to it. Grab a few packs of M&M's and some tabloid magazines, and take a seat in the waiting area. If the pharmacist asks if you are being helped, hold up the M&M's and say, "These are helping! But if you have something stronger . . ."

THE LOCAL ORGANIC VEGAN RESTAURANT

Regardless of their mood, the ultrahealthy just know how to look sad. And if you like the unsatisfying feeling that a dairy-free, wheat-free, gluten-free "tuna" melt leaves you with, then you'll love paying thirty-five dollars for it.

MY DEPRESSION WAS BORN ON:

_____

DAY   MONTH   YEAR

(THIS IS THE DAY YOU FIRST NOTICED YOUR DEPRESSION.)

IT WAS CREATED BY:

_____

(E.G., GENES, BREAKUP, FAILURE, HORRIBLE BOSS, BAD
LUCK, STRESS, RECESSION, CIVIL WAR, PULLED HAMSTRING.)

MY DEPRESSION
GOES BY THE NAME:

_____

(E.G., HUMILIATING DEFEAT, DOMINEERING PARENT,
SLEEP DEPRIVATION, SQUASHED DREAMS,
CYBER EXHAUSTION, CAN'T FIX OTHERS, ETC.)

FAQ

Q: If I'm not Jewish, can I still be depressed?

A: Yes, but only if your mother was.

Q: Does being depressed make me smarter?

A: Buying this book does.

Q: Am I allowed to laugh?

A: Certainly. But after you must take an audible sigh of resignation that says, *That was nice, but now I must return to the hell I've been sentenced to.*

Q: What if I have kids?

A: You can make them depressed too. A chip off the old Zoloft!

Q: What if I have parents?

A: Why do you think you're depressed?

Q: Does depression have a cure?

A: No, but you could listen to The Cure.

Q: Can I drink alcohol?

A: Yes, but not after 9AM, and avoid fun drinks, like appletinis and piña coladas.

Q: Do I need to be an artist or writer?

A: It's up to you, but any creation must be judged before completing, deemed unworthy of your talent (or depression), and passionately destroyed.

Q: Are there any motivational speakers I can listen to?

A: Nick Drake.

Q: Can I be poor and depressed?

A: Yes, that's just called poverty. Unfortunately, poverty has no DSM-5 diagnostic code.

Q: How many things can I hate about myself at once?

A: Start counting.

DEPRESSION MILESTONES

Your therapist knows your tale of woe by heart, but have you ever written it down? Really stared it in the face like she has? It's bad. It's boring. It's yours. Take a moment to share it with yourself.

Use the blank lines below to record your thoughts and feelings about a given milestone. Paste in any relevant ephemera, mementos, or photos, especially ones where your smile is concealing your pain.

BRINGING DEPRESSION HOME
The first time your little bundle of despair appeared, you didn't know it was depression, did you? You thought you just needed to rest and refuel. The moment you realized it was here to stay, was it panic? Peace? Or the start of a new blog?

_____

_____

_____

_____

_____

_____

_____

_____

_____

_____

_____

DEPRESSION'S FIRST FOOD

Does your depression have a favorite food? Does it leave you full but empty? Disgusted? Ashamed? Do they know you by name at the gas station convenience store? Have you ever thrown your shame cake in the trash but gone back for more?

_____

_____

_____

_____

_____

_____

_____

DEPRESSION DIET

Have you ever been so depressed you can't even think about eating? How awesome is that?! Perhaps in the past you'd thought, _If I could drop weight without feeling hungry all day, I'd be happy._ Well you actually can, except for that happy part.

_____

_____

_____

_____

_____

_____

_____

DEPRESSION'S MINDLESS ESCAPES
What was depression's first mode of distraction? Alcohol? Music? Binge eating? Binge watching? Perhaps there is a war documentary, a PBS twelve-part miniseries, or a weekend marathon of *Forensic Files*. Endless drama to absorb and reality to ignore.

_____

_____

_____

_____

_____

_____

_____

FIRST TIME YOUR DEPRESSION SLEPT THROUGH THE NIGHT. AND THE WEEKEND.
The first time depression sleeps through the weekend is when you begin to sense life can actually be ignored. What—if anything—finally woke you? Did you stay awake or roll right back over?

_____

_____

_____

_____

_____

_____

_____

DEPRESSION'S FIRST AND LAST WORDS

The only thing more important than depression's first words are depression's last words. You know, the ones that drove your friends away. Did you leave drunken voicemail messages, write angry texts, or deliver broken poetry via poetry slam? What was your most sad and pathetic line?

_____

_____

_____

_____

_____

_____

_____

IT GROWS SO FAST! DON'T FORGET TO RECORD ALL OF DEPRESSION'S OTHER MILESTONES!

➤ First time I thought I might have to move back in with my parents

➤ First time I asked my brother for money

➤ First time getting evicted

➤ First time assembling facts as though they were simply random misfortunes instead of a number of disasters I brought on myself

➤ And so many more!

GETTING STARTED WRAP-UP

Did you get the sweatpants? Of course not, you're depressed. Anyway, what you have on hand will do quite nicely. Are you sure you haven't done this before? You catch on quickly.

Now that you've had the opportunity to explore depression's landscape and attractions, you hold the pieces (albeit broken) for your new beginning. You have some places to go, people to contact, and supplies for a daily practice. Perhaps you've not yet established your daily routine. That's okay. When it comes to depression, inconsistency is key.

Depression is a process—it takes time. Be steadfast, continue to review, wallow, nap, and practice your all-or-nothings. In the next chapter, you'll learn about building a solid depression foundation, one that ensures depression will endure. If you don't feel ready, don't worry. That just means you're not ready for anything. Except chapter two.

BUILDING YOUR DEPRESSION FOUNDATION

In order to achieve a depression that lasts, you need a proper depression foundation, one that is uneven, cracked, and sinking. The linchpin to success lies in your ability to avoid present-day thinking. This includes the moment. You'll want to avoid the moment at all costs.

That is because regret about the past and anxiety about the future are the key emotional drivers at the core of any quality depression. As you begin, you'll become intimately acquainted with each of these feelings, but before long you'll be introduced to a whole new world of crippling emotions.

Balancing regret and anxiety produces the ideal soil to plant your depression roots. In years to come, you'll have a steady growth of doubt and distrust blooming in every direction. Over time, it will become difficult to know where depression ends and you begin. What you once called a slump, you will now call destiny.

CONGRATULATIONS! YOU ARE ON YOUR WAY.

REGRET: LEARNING TO LIVE IN THE PAST

Wow, you've made some bad choices! This is hardly news. Regret acknowledges your current life for what it is: the aftermath of poor choices.

Regret analysis falls into two basic categories:
  1. The action you took.
  2. The action you failed to take.

Unwise choices have led to walks of shame, high-interest loans, totaled cars, bars from which you've been banned, and a list of sexual partners you had to contact with positive test results. At this point, your best hope is that nothing was captured on video.

Then there are the actions you failed to take: calling on birthdays, registering your invention, flossing, reading warning labels, and contacting past partners with positive test results.

Regret serves as a reminder that you do not have good instincts, some styles are for celebrities only, and when you dance like no one is watching, you offend the people who are.

For the next few pages—as we examine that which you've neglected, broken, and left in ruins—just sit back, relax, and don't touch anything!

FAMILY REGRET

Family is great for living in the past! That's because despite the years spent transforming into the person you are today, your family can tear it all down within mere minutes. Sometimes with just a single glance.

It's as though they lie in wait for the tiniest echo of a past transgression, so they can reminisce about all your greatest hits—those embarrassing memories you were once so ashamed of. It's okay. You're an adult now. You can speak up and set those boundaries you learned in therapy. They'll think it's hilarious.

When you insist you've changed, your family lets you know that it's okay not to. That mortifying attribute you've tried to conceal all these years is in actuality your essence. It's what makes you *you*, and there's nothing wrong with it (which is why they're making fun of it).

Know that your family is not laughing with you, they are laughing at you. It's not that they're better. Your presence just gives them a chance to feel better. Don't get upset with your family. They made you exactly who they needed you to be.

THE PRECIOUS MOMENTS OF REGRET

So far, you've kept regret safely hidden away. But what if I could offer you a beautiful case in which to display your regrets? Before saying, "Hell, no!" let's unwrap one of these treasures. Just look at the detail: crafted through rumination, expertly chiseled to define the sharpest edges of your stupid mistakes. As the years pass, you're bound to come across regrets you didn't even know you had. You've amassed considerable collections. A few highlights:

> ➤ The Stupid Things I Did
> ➤ The Stupid Things I Said
> ➤ The Successful People I Should Have Stayed in Touch With
> ➤ The Why Did I Shout, "Take a Video!"

Don't let these valuable treasures be lost. As a bonus, each Precious Moment of Regret comes with a certificate authenticating your ability to fail in most situations. Imagine weekends home alone polishing and arranging each Regret. Consider passing them on to your children and grandchildren, who will sit around the table imploring, "Who does a reverse mortgage?"

While taking stock of regret, be sure to tell yourself that, given the chance, you would do things differently the next time. But when you see your display full of duplicates, triplicates, and even infinicates—many of which were added this week—reality dawns: no, no you would not have.

SPERM:
I Should've gone down
the tube less taken.

EGG:
I shouldn't have
waited this long.
My biological
clock is ticking.

ZYGOTE:
Why do I
look like a
potato! This
can't be good
genetic code.

Child:
I should've listened
to Mom and gone to
the bathroom before
we left the house.

EMBRYO:
Splitting makes two
of us. These are going
to be tight quarters.

Baby:
Oh, that didn't belong
in my mouth. No, that
doesn't either.... how
about this? Nope.

Teen:
HOW long does
shoplifting stay
on my record?

YOUNG ADULT:
urns out a philosophy
egree does not pay
or itself.

THE HUMAN LIFE CYCLE OF REGRET

Each regret was born under a unique set of circumstances. Some regrets emerge with no assistance whatsoever, while others grow from a lack of information, opportunity, or proper connections. Among all your regrets there is one unifying theory of misfortune, and that is y-o-u.

ADULT:
I do! I do? NO I didn't.
Undo, undo, Control-Alt-Delete.

SENIOR:
I should have been kinder to others or purchased long-term-care insurance.

CORPSE:
Wait, I didn't clear history.

TIME'S UP!
(REGRET BOOSTERS)

By the time you reach middle age, regret is second nature. Meanwhile, opportunities to change, reinvent yourself, or earn vindication are quickly vanishing. At this point, you have a better chance of collecting the inheritance of a Nigerian prince than receiving even a modicum of success or notoriety. In your heart you know it's too late for anything except a midnight snack.

IT'S TOO LATE!
To be a child prodigy, a child star, or be described as someone "wise beyond her years."

IT'S TOO LATE!
To join the Peace Corps, join a sorority, join a rock band, or recover the pain-free movement of your joints.

IT'S TOO LATE!
To invent Facebook, buy Google, cash in on Enron.

IT'S TOO LATE!
To be a journalist, be an explorer, or learn the New Math.

IT'S TOO LATE!
To save your gums, save your soul, save the whales, save for retirement.

IT'S TOO LATE!
To bring peace to the Middle East, bring joy to the world, bring it full circle.

IT'S TOO LATE!
To preserve your youth, revive your liver, purchase a mausoleum, find friends who will visit you at the mausoleum, find friends who will visit you now.

FIND YOUR DEPRESSION MATCH

Regret not only creates the foundation for a strong and lasting depression, it allows you to usher in even more crippling feelings. Regardless of which type you choose, there is an unattached crippling emotion just waiting to knock you off your feet. In fact, a special few have been asking about you...

GUILT

There you are! No, you're not really late. I just thought you would have called. Don't worry about it. I've been looking for someone just like you! However, I must admit most of my past partners have been moms. Of course I'm open to all types—Catholics, Jews, or anyone who views the fulfillment of their own needs as selfish. You should contact me if you're sure your best isn't good enough.

JEALOUSY

I'm a great partner for a twin, a stage mother, or anyone with a long-standing rivalry. I spend a lot of time on Facebook. I just like to see what everyone is up to. I went to high school with some really impressive people. Trust me, you certainly wouldn't have known it then. Contact me if you're interested or if you just want to compare notes. I think we'd be great together. Better than a lot of other couples that I know. That's for sure!

RESENTMENT

Oh, hey there. Maybe we could go out for drinks sometime when I'm not working late, doing more than my share, or seething? I am open to whatever activity you insist we try. Afterward, I promise—if you're the guy or gal I think you are—you'll be looking at the receipt wondering why you offered to pay. If so, we have a bright future ahead where we'll brood over the brighter future we deserved.

EMPTINESS

I'm open to meeting someone who's been recently drained by a lengthy divorce battle, is caring for an ailing loved one, or is stuck in a continuous work cycle with no reprieve on the horizon. I'll admit I like to start new relationships when I've got nothing to give. Texting with me is like waiting for a washed-out message in a bottle. If you feel like you're missing something but are unsure what, let me *not* complete you.

EMBARRASSMENT

Hello. Let me tell you a little bit about myself. I love sheer fabrics, slippery wet floors, and my favorite color is beet red. My ideal partner is overconfident, loud, and lacks coordination. I'm especially partial to a big smile with food trapped between the teeth. A perfect date includes anything in bright, natural light, like a romantic walk on the beach, where I can see your acne scars. Regardless of what we do, I promise a wonderful end to the evening by whispering sweet nothings like, "Your fly is down." Get drunk and message me!

DETACHMENT

I'm really glad you looked at my profile. The fact that you never wrote or showed any sign of your presence makes me think you just might be the one. I like to give my partners plenty of space. I'm seeking someone who enjoys a long-distance relationship or an emotionally distant one. You can rest assured that when you feel alone, that is me there by your side. You should definitely contact me if you're someone who might forget why you contacted me to begin with.

ANXIETY: FEAR THE FUTURE!

Feeling overwhelmed by reality? Secretly, you take refuge in your future: the idea of something happening by luck, effort, inheritance, or a lottery ticket that would catapult you to success.

Screw that. In order to continue laying your depression foundation, you need to unfriend the future and embrace anxiety. Anxiety is overwhelming stress, uncertainty, and a feeling of impending doom. Sound familiar? You are really close.

STEP 1. DISMANTLE HOPE

In the past, you've turned to your dreams and aspirations to quell present-day dissatisfaction. No more.

Dreams and aspirations require initiative. Achievement is the result of accumulated effort. Do you know how much effort *effort* takes? You don't have that kind of energy. Your body can barely digest dairy much less create its own energy.

STEP 2. CHOKE UNDER PRESSURE

What do you have coming up that your boss, mother-in-law, or government requires of you? Have you waited till the last minute to take care of this matter? Good. Is there no one who can fulfill this requirement but you? Excellent. Does failure spell the end of your career, relationship, sense of worth?

Count the steps that stand between you and successful completion. Don't take action. Avoidance is the key to anxiety success. The discomfort zone is where you want to be.

STEP 3. TRANSFORM DOUBT TO DOOM

Uncertainty can be scary, but you can make it even scarier by imagining disastrous outcomes beyond your control. It is like a Choose Your Own Adventure book except you get to Choose Your Own Tragedy. Exciting!

There are so many tragedies to choose from. Just watch the news and find a story that speaks to you. Perhaps it'll be a freak accident, E.coli, or a series of shark sightings.

As you get caught tighter in anxiety's grip, you may notice a slowing in cognition and memory. Whenever you can, blame others, take shallow breaths, and grab a few more cups of coffee. With these worries, you will be up all night, and that's when you've succeeded beyond your wildest nightmares.

ANXIETY BOOST #1

FEAR YOUR FUTURE

DREAM CATCHER

DREAM
RELEASER

ANxIETY BOOST #2

LOSE PERSPECTIVE

HALF FULL

HALF EMPTY

MEDLEY OF DESPAIR: WORD-FIND GAME

```
D  I  S  C  O  N  N  E  C  T  E  D  J  D  K  T  T  Q  N  G
E  T  W  R  E  C  K  E  D  X  K  E  Y  Y  B  V  P  X  B  O
S  J  D  E  J  E  C  T  E  D  F  J  Q  Q  S  R  I  J  A  D
P  M  E  C  R  U  S  H  E  D  A  C  H  Y  M  F  T  K  Z  F
E  M  P  O  E  L  F  M  O  R  T  I  F  I  E  D  I  O  D  O
R  G  L  L  M  F  M  E  M  P  T  Y  F  C  S  G  F  W  H  R
A  L  E  L  A  U  O  L  Q  Y  T  F  Q  U  L  Q  U  O  O  S
T  O  T  A  B  T  U  A  Z  D  O  E  S  B  U  S  L  E  D  A
E  O  E  P  A  I  R  N  F  B  R  C  Q  L  G  O  Q  B  E  K
H  M  D  S  N  L  N  C  M  F  M  K  U  A  G  J  F  E  S  E
M  Y  K  E  D  E  F  H  O  N  E  L  X  I  I  N  B  G  T  N
O  V  E  D  O  K  U  O  R  B  N  E  Z  Q  S  A  R  O  R  B
T  C  P  I  N  Z  L  L  O  R  T  S  A  S  H  Y  S  N  O  D
J  O  Y  L  E  S  S  Y  S  D  E  S  T  I  T  U  T  E  Y  R
K  T  E  B  D  V  B  O  E  Q  D  C  U  V  A  R  B  H  E  W
A  P  O  W  E  R  L  E  S  S  Q  F  Y  S  P  K  A  E  D  E
Q  S  E  S  Y  M  G  D  E  F  E  A  T  E  D  M  B  G  U  C
Q  W  K  S  K  L  B  I  O  R  L  O  P  T  K  H  T  S  I  P
Y  G  M  L  F  O  R  L  O  R  N  I  T  W  E  P  V  S  U  C
C  R  E  S  T  F  A  L  L  E  N  O  F  A  T  K  T  H  R  L
```

MELANCHOLY
DEJECTED
CRESTFALLEN
FORLORN
MORTIFIED
DEFEATED
MOROSE
FECKLESS
FUTILE
DESPERATE
PITIFUL
JOYLESS
TRAGIC
COLLAPSED
MOURNFUL

ACHY
ABANDONED
GLOOMY
TORMENTED
SLUGGISH
DESTROYED
DISCONNECTED
WOEBEGONE
POWERLESS
WRECKED
GODFORSAKEN
DESTITUTE
CRUSHED
EMPTY
DEPLETED

MEDLEY OF DESPAIR: ANSWERS

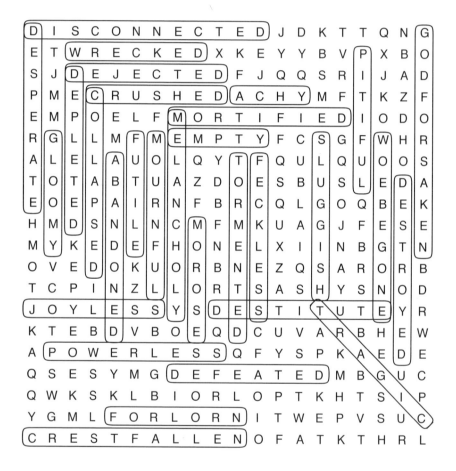

GOODNIGHT GLOOM
A WORRIER'S BEDTIME STORY

In a small hoarder's room.
There was a cracked iPhone.
And a life in ruin.
And a picture of a priest running off with the groom.

There were bills unpaid.
A credit downgrade.
Six Ritalin.
One big tailspin.

Radio warnings of a midmorning rush.
An insomniac rolling over, whispering "hush."

Goodnight doom.
Goodnight gloom.
Goodnight meteors that fall from the sky with a smashing boom.

Goodnight debt.
Goodnight fret.
Goodnight worry.
Goodnight fury.
Goodnight numbness in hands with a tingling sensation.
Goodnight internal bleeding or ulceration.

Goodnight fries.
Goodnight lies.
Goodnight chest pain.
Goodnight cocaine.
Goodnight new suspicious mole.
Goodnight fear of passing out and losing control.

Goodnight 5K lost to online betting.
Goodnight critical reminder I am now forgetting.

Goodnight drunken text.
Goodnight undersexed.
Goodnight IRS audit and tax evasion.
Goodnight criminal investigation.

6AM. It is time to wake and face the day that she dreads.
But now she is tired and ready for bed.
Goodnight toxic air.
Goodnight things out to get me everywhere.

DEPRESSION FOUNDATION WRAP-UP

Frankly, I'm surprised you're still here. Good job! Throughout this chapter, you've tried to make sense of the past. You've examined regrets. You've looked to the future, hoping it would all become clear. (Of course, it didn't.) And, finally, you mingled with some of depression's best pals.

So here's where you stand (even though you're probably lying down): stuck right where you are! It's what we in the depress biz call paralysis. Mornings you are paralyzed. During the day you feel boxed-in. And as the sun sets over the horizon, you feel a longing, a lack of meaning (also called existential angst and futility). You're home.

As you move forward on your depression adventure, continue to bounce between the past and the future. Over time, it will become second nature. It's like the *Karate Kid*—wax on, wax off. Before you know it, you'll beat the smile out of happiness.

IT'S A SAD, SAD, SAD, SAD WORLD

You've acquired the depression basics and laid your emotional foundation of regret and anxiety. Terrific! Sadly though, these negative thoughts aren't going to sustain themselves, at least not at first. To maintain progress, you'll need to create an environment that feeds negativity—one that incubates despair and shields you from hope. That way, you'll be able to quickly and efficiently produce thoughts to keep you depressed and defeat happiness.

The following chapter will be your system to do just that. It'll help you avoid life, repel others, and work with a range of techniques to keep you escalating toward self-sabotage. Consider it your own personal wrecking ball: it's where your inner child star hits adolescence. It's where you open a gas can in Hell. Have you ever seen a car back up from an accident into another car? Yes! That's the sweet spot.

THOUGHTS & FEELINGS

Let's begin with your pathetic thoughts. Perhaps there are some days you still feel pretty upbeat. That's okay! Luckily, depression is a cheap, renewable energy source, and each day a continuous stream of negative thoughts will be rolling in. To ensure these notions can withstand opposing elements, like smiles, children, and morning talk shows, you will need to leave behind thoughts of a flimsy nature.

For each negative thought you have, ask yourself: is this fact or opinion?

The answer is always the same.

When it's a negative thought, it's a fact. When it's a hopeful thought, it's simply your opinion. It's so easy, even a child could do it—a very angry, negative, horrible child.

NEG THOUGHTS = ☹
POS THOUGHTS = ☹

THOUGHT-EVALUATION SYSTEM

STEP 1				
Supply thought	I feel ugly today. ○	I am helpful. ○	I can't pay my bills. ○	I'm funny. ○
STEP 2				
Conversion: convert negative thoughts to fact	I am ugly.	⇩	I am worthless.	⇩
STEP 3				
Conversion: invert positive thoughts to negative	⇩	I am destructive.	⇩	I am sad.
STEP 4				
Add "everyone knows" before each statement	Everyone knows I am ugly.	Everyone knows I am destructive.	Everyone knows I am worthless.	Everyone knows I am sad.
STEP 3				
Include your impact on the world	I am ruining everyone's dinner.	I'm destroying myself and others.	I am a drain on global resources.	I make the whole world cry.
STEP 4				
Now add death	I am so ugly someone will look at me, have a stroke, and die.	One of my destructive actions will set off a chain of events that will cause everyone in my vicinity to fall into a sinkhole and die.	I'm going to die broke.	I cause the kind of heartbreak that makes people stop eating, washing, or trying. They fold themselves up, shrivel, and die.
STEP 5 (OPTIONAL)				
Take a creative leap! Add your own dramatic flair and see how far you can go!	I am a murderer. I sour milk. I make E.coli. I should hang a construction sign around my neck that reads Pardon My Appearance.	I am responsible for global warming, fender benders, unfoldable fitted bed sheets, rudeness, and elevator doors that close just as you arrive.	My death would go entirely unnoticed were it not for my debtors and the stench of decomposition.	I am why small children cry, toys break, and wi-fi signals disappear.

DAILY NEGATIONS

You'll want to begin each day with Daily Negations, short phrases designed to reignite doubt, throw you into a tailspin, and stop positive action in its tracks. Delightful! You can easily memorize and recite your negations throughout the day. With each recitation, they'll begin to seep into your mind and guide all of your choices. Read one or two lines at a time upon waking. Let them sink in and set off alarm bells, then crawl back to bed.

What your father said about you is true.

That's an ugly shirt.

You should drink more.

You'll never be able to prove that you
are smarter than your boss.

You shouldn't be around children.

You are not memorable.

Feel that person behind you? That's just your butt.

Your computer knows exactly what you are trying to do. It just
doesn't like you. In fact, it thinks you're an idiot.
(So does the printer.)

People do overcome tough breaks like yours,
but they're different, better people.

Observe what in your life is working. Well, that was quick.

It's not bad lighting. That's what you look like.

Go ahead! Learn a new language.
Be unfunny in two languages!

You are a miracle! But you were probably God's last
one that day. Clearly, he was rushing out of the
office and didn't quite finish.

Without Facebook, no one would remember your birthday.

Open new doors to life! That's "pull" not "push," you idiot.

Your friends invite you to hang out when
no one else is available. You're an alternate.
Probably the third alternate.

Your plant didn't die. It took the easy way out.

Everyone knows you're not busy. You just waste time.

Your life is exactly where it should be.
You're actually performing far ahead of your abilities.

The doctor reads your chart and laughs.

When someone says, "You look hot,"
they mean you're sweating.

Remember the fifth-grade teacher who convinced you
that you had talent? He meant at a fifth-grade level.

There's someone for everyone. You challenge that theory.

FINDING YOUR DEPRESSED POSE

Inhabiting a pose of inner turmoil cannot be taught; it can only be felt. It takes patience, self-absorption, commitment, and (fortunately for you) no motivation. Once perfected, a pose can be held for years at a time. With such prolonged stillness, how can one know if she has achieved a depression pose or merely fallen asleep? Exactly!

Try the poses below, pick a favorite, and stick with it!

THE SLOTH
After weeks of sleep, you've decided you need something—a drink, a snack, a new menu—to continue subsisting. Using only your forearms, slowly shimmy across the floor to reach the relief or nourishment you desire. Use your journey to second-guess whether the pain is worth it.

CATERPILLAR POSE
When a caterpillar falls from a tree, it rolls into a ball to protect itself from the impact. Re-enact this moment by curling up your torso and tucking in your head. You will now be shielded from the harsh impact of life and from people who are happier than you (which is everyone).

THE HANGMAN CLASSIC

You've seen this on airplanes:
a napping passenger's head,
unsupported, circles above the
body like a marble in a roulette
wheel. When you become
a real pro, you'll be able to do
this at the dinner table with
your family.

THE AFGHAN BURRITO

Roll yourself from one corner
of your blanket to the other,
tucking in any loose edges.
You're not going for mere
newborn-swaddling here; go
full on Eastern-bloc orphan-
age. If you feel stifled, stuck,
and abandoned, you're doing
it right. If you are dreaming of
your next bottle-feeding and the
bottle is filled with vodka, you
nailed it!

CHIP OFF THE OLD CHIPS

A squishy surface like a
pillow, couch, or bed acts as an
automated food-delivery system.
When you need nourishment,
open your mouth, pressing your
chin ever so slightly into the
cushy surface beside you. With
help from gravity, the chips,
cake crumbs, or other starches
of choice simply fall in,
satisfying your hunger.

THE FLOP

Exactly as it sounds. Generally
reserved for those who've
returned home after interacting
with the outside world. Don't
bother to undress. Position
yourself at the base of the bed
and flop forward, facedown.
Now stay!

HOW TO LEAVE THINGS UNFINISHED

Avoidance is an essential skill of the depressed. Getting started is the hardest part. The good news is that's all you need to do! Review the sample below and when you feel ready, and not a moment sooner, feel free to take no action.

STEP 1.
Have brilliant idea!

STEP 2.
Write lots of notes about idea. Important: make notes in a variety of spots—napkins, your phone, backs of bank statements.

STEP 3.
Promise yourself you won't share idea with others for fear it will be stolen. Announce to everyone: "I have this brilliant life-changing idea." Then share it anyway for early praise.

STEP 4.
Set goal to complete plan by dinnertime tonight.

STEP 5.
Assemble all your notes. Of course, there will be one or two you won't be able to find. You're unsure what they were because you're a creative person who experiences altered states when creating. But you know these were the keys to your vision.

STEP 6.
Make a file.

STEP 7.
Make a list of action items and next steps. Notice something just doesn't feel right.

STEP 8.
Call a friend.

STEP 9.
Have a snack.

STEP 10.
Spend two hours searching for your lucky pen.

STEP 11.
Make a list of office supplies you'll need.

STEP 12.
Rearrange your office according to the laws of feng shui.

STEP 13A.—13F.
Look up the laws of feng shui.
Look up the news of the day.
Look up horoscope.
Look up ex's horoscope.
Look up pointers on focus, willpower, and success.

STEP 14.
Relax. Have a drink. You can't work when you're this tense.

STEP 15.
Vow not to go on the internet. But first check WebMD for that weird bump you've got on your tongue.

STEP 15A.
Realize you are dying and must say goodbye to your loved ones.

STEP 15B.
Seek the opinion of a medical professional.

STEP 15C.
Get a second opinion. Go for a third, fourth, and fifth.

STEP 16.
Seek trauma counseling. Accept that you've just had a big scare and are not well enough to create anything. Failing to complete this project does not take away from the fact that you are a genius.

STEP 17.
Make a list of all of your other great ideas. Circle those better than the one you're working on.

STEP 18.
Realize there are no fairies, no workshop elves assembling our ideas, but secretly continue to hold out hope that divine intervention will occur.

STEP 19.
When you feel the fleeting pull of action or encouragement, breathe it out. Let it go. Remember if a brilliant idea exists in your mind. That's good enough.

STEP 20.
Finally, and this is the most important step, you'll want to consider . . .

DEPRESSION ON A BUDGET

Like a city under siege, your relationships, car, physical health, and finances will begin to crumble in rapid succession. While this provides the texture and depth for a supreme depressive experience, you may find you lack the financial resources necessary to feed the cycle of decay. Fortunately, we live in a DIY age, and with this handy chart, even a scrappy person like yourself can assemble a kit of everything needed to live the best depressed life possible.

DEPRESSION ESSENTIAL	DIY REPLACEMENT	SAVINGS
PSYCHOTHERAPIST	Try a television therapist. For example, The Learning Channel's *Hoarders Buried Alive* has some wonderful ones. There's also Dr. Drew, Dr. Phil, and Dr. Pepper. Or forget the therapist and just try seeing a psycho (available on Craigslist). Less effective but more fun!	$100 per week
PSYCHIATRIST	Consult your local high school drug dealer or simply raid your friend's medicine cabinet. You know which friend.	$300 per month + Rx cost
XANAX	Cheap Chinese takeout, washed down with a generic over-the-counter sleep aid.	$50 per month
AMPHETAMINES	Combine equal portions energy drink, red licorice, and daytime cough syrup.	$55 per month (and you won't need food)
TOXIC RELATIONSHIP	Instead of a healthy relationship, try slutting it up in group therapy or at a local church social. They have free coffee, baked goods, and participants are required to listen and not judge. Their souls are riding on it.	Thirty years of mediocrity you can achieve on your own.
BINGE EATING	1. Costco samples 2. Time-share seminars 3. Wakes/funerals 4. Holiday Inn breakfasts	$25 per week
BINGE TELEVISION	If you have cable, tune in to a marathon weekend of any reality show where you get to feel at once disgusted by and superior to the human race. If you don't have cable, "volunteer" at a nursing home and befriend a senior with the same viewing preferences as yours.	$100 per month
ALCOHOL	Try cough syrup or homemade moonshine. For the romantically inclined, date a Russian.	$140 per month
GOOD POT	If you don't have access to good pot, date a dealer. Or just settle for bad pot.	$300 per week
BAD POT	Catnip!	$40 per week
	TOTAL ANNUAL SAVINGS	$30,000.00+

PSYCHIATRIC EVALUATION:
Good Grief

PATIENT INFORMATION

Patient Name: Charlie Brown
Affectionately Known As: Chuck
Unaffectionately Known As: Blockhead
Lived: October 2, 1950-Indefinitely (which makes goal-setting har...
Lived Happily: Never (but his dog did).
Profession: Protagonist. Birdcage Liner.

Career Highlights:
Ice Capades
Macy's Thanksgiving Day Parade
Lunchboxes

Career Lowlights:
Commercials for MetLife Insurance. (As one who doesn't age, grow, or drive, Mr. Brown never got comfortable with his role as a representative for life, disability, and car insurance.)

CASE HISTORY

Symptoms:
- Appears to never change his shirt.
- Early hair loss or lack of hair growth.
- Patient feels his life has been written for him.
- Has difficulty waking up in the morning and goes to sleep feeling slightly smudged.
- Feels terrible sense of déjà vu every holiday season.

Previous Treatment:
Was treated by a Dr. Lucy. Discontinued treatment because she didn't take his health insurance. Turns out MetLife only covers dea...

Risk Factors:
- Inability to age chronologically.
- Cannot understand adults.
- Does not feel understood by dog.
- No access to eraser.

Recommended Treatment:

- Stop hoping.
- Stop kicking football.
- Join a different gang.

DEPRESSION TRAVEL GUIDE

Fortunately, depression can thrive in nearly any climate, though it's best known for its work indoors. Below is a brief overview of cities with rich depressing ecosystems that will support, sustain, and contribute to your depressing life. There, you will be surrounded by others like yourself. Luckily, they won't want to talk to you either.

CHICAGO

LOS ANGELES

PHOENIX

NEW YORK

SEATTLE

FRANCE

YOUR HOMETOWN

PERKS OF BEING DEPRESSED IN
SEATTLE

1. Sleep all day without the help of blackout curtains.

GLUTEN, DAIRY, GMO FREE

2. With all this gluten-free, dairy-free, GMO-free food, swallowing your feelings will seem like a delicacy.

3. It's the only city where long johns count as lingerie.

4. "Busy Composting" is considered a perfectly valid excuse for not having sex.

5. With all this rain, your tears will be indistinguishable.

6. Discover ninety-four varieties of flannel out of your price range.

7. Your suffering will never compare to that of the environment.

REI

8. Shop at REI without the hassle of adventure.

9. Feel the wet damp ghost of Kurt Cobain.

SIGN OUR PETITION

10. Each day you'll be asked to sign a petition for a cause more tragic than yours.

PERKS OF BEING DEPRESSED IN
LOS ANGELES

1. The only thing more important than who you know is what you're allergic to.

2. Everyone will want to hear about your depression long enough to tell you about their secret, amazing recovery. (Hint: it was loving themselves when no one else would. And clearly no one else would.)

3. Suddenly high school doesn't seem so clique-y.

Screenplay

4. Working on a screenplay is a perfectly acceptable answer to what you've been doing for the past twenty years.

5. You'll find out 80% of life is showing up, but the other 180% is finding parking.

6. It's the ideal place to date someone who really takes an interest in the person sitting behind you.

7. Compared to what you're paying for smoothies, pot seems really cheap.

8. If you can't find a new religion, you can make one up.

9. If you're running late, you'll always be on time.

10. No need to concern yourself with tragic world events—or any news for that matter—until they're made into a blockbuster hit.

PERKS OF BEING DEPRESSED IN
NEW YORK CITY

2. The only thing bigger than your pile of resentment is your pile of menus.

1. No need to yell at yourself—other people will do it for you.

3. Living in the same apartment for twenty years is seen as an accomplishment.

4. Enjoy new activities, like counting how many places smell like pee.

5. Say goodbye to paranoia. You are in fact a target.

8. 2 AM pizza is considered a nutritional staple.

6. You are never expected to have guests in your home—other than the eight roommates who already live there.

7. Visit downtown, where your disturbing behavior is performance art.

9. Start spreading the news: you can't make it anywhere!

10. At the end of an un-showered month, you'll smell better than New Jersey.

PERKS OF BEING DEPRESSED IN
CHICAGO

1. With 19 miles of lakefront paths buried beneath seventeen feet of snow, there's always a reason to stay indoors.

2. Between deep-dish pizza, Chicago-style hot dogs, and Italian beef, letting yourself go never tasted so good.

4. If you want to give up completely, Detroit is right next door!

5. You'll win more than the Cubs.

3. With all this street violence, suicide requires zero planning.

7. When the doors to life slam in your face, you can blame the wind.

6. With 36 annual parades, your exercise regime has the alcoholism already built in.

10. Take heart Chicagoans, you will prevail—even Hemingway left to kill himself.

8. With a checkered past like yours, people will call you mayor.

9. Join a support group like the famed Second City, and you can musically improvise depression.

PERKS OF BEING DEPRESSED IN
PHOENIX

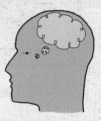

1. When people ask if you're depressed, you get to say: "Yes, but it's a dry depression."

2. Finally, a cure for P.T.S.D.! Even traumatic memories will get bored and leave.

3. You won't attempt suicide once you've test-driven the temperatures of hell.

4. With so many funerals, there's always a place to cry.

5. Relive junior high! Take a class at Arizona State.

6. People will believe you when you claim your tears are just sweat.

7. With so many venomous snakes, spiders, and scorpions, it may not be necessary to take your own life. They'll do it for you!

8. Experience Vegas without all that pesky fun.

9. Discover a place where you can conceal feelings as well as weapons.

10. Hey, chin up! Next to this state border, you won't seem so insecure.

PERKS OF BEING DEPRESSED IN
YOUR HOMETOWN

3. Discover the people from your past are just as boring as their Facebook posts.

1. At least now you have an excuse for not dating the most popular kid in school. It's a felony.

2. When asked why you're going home, explain that you weren't interested in going big.

5. Discover your romantic life is the perfect match for your old twin bed.

4. Thank your scout leader for teaching you to survive in the wild. Now ask if he could teach you to survive in a junior one bedroom.

8. Track down your old hot babysitter to find out what she charges now.

6. You'll feel your age when surrounded by those who actually know it.

7. Maybe your drunk uncle will seem less annoying when you get drunk with him.

4. Fix your parents' computer and feel like a tech wizard!

10. Find out if depression gets you out of doing the dishes.

PERKS OF BEING DEPRESSED IN
FRANCE

1. Don't talk to anyone for days. Call it your Marcel Marceau impression.

2. Take note from Descartes: "I think, therefore I am depressed."

3. Tell people you are not depressed. You are Les misérables.

4. If you take a selfie next to the Mona Lisa, you'll look cheery.

5. Break bread with the French and discover it <u>is</u> your metabolism.

6. It's the only place where idling in bed all day drinking wine is <u>not</u> considered alcoholism.

7. Your depression isn't chronic, it's déjà vu.

8. The drugs you've consumed may actually qualify you for the Tour de France.

9. Discover there's no shame in surrendering.

10. You're supposed to die penniless in a garret.

I RUINED IT

Catastrophes of the past inform your future. Create a FAIL journal to gather data, so you may get a complete picture of the damage done. Such information reminds you to set aside your "inspired ideas" in favor of activities more suited to your aptitude and disposition, like napping through an important work meeting, studying *US Weekly*, or agreeing with expert advice while visualizing yourself doing the exact opposite.

Below are prompts that will get you started on creating your very own record of all the ways you've already defeated yourself.

Three people who hate me with good reason:

_____

_____

_____

Pets I neglected:

_____

_____

_____

Children I lied to:

_____

_____

_____

Grandparents I never called:

_____

_____

_____

Exes I dumped who went onto someone better:

_____

_____

_____

Activities that disqualify me from political office:

_____

_____

_____

Internet searches that ban me from law enforcement:

_____

_____

_____

Three friends my parents like more than me and would
easily trade me for:

_____

_____

_____

Chemicals I've ingested that will likely affect future offspring:

_____

_____

_____

Jobs I performed drunk or mentally impaired:

_____

_____

_____

Activities my parents heavily invested in that I quit:

_____

_____

_____

Four game-changing moments I blew:

_____

_____

_____

Clothing I hang onto hoping to miraculously fit into it again:

_____

_____

_____

Five things that would get me fired if discovered by my boss:

_____

_____

_____

What I suspect people say about me when I leave the room
and why it is true:

_____

_____

_____

Friends who grew up with far fewer advantages who went
on to greater success:

_____

_____

_____

Items discarded because I'd rather toss them than clean them:

_____

_____

_____

Projects I started but never finished:

_____

_____

_____

SAD, SAD WORLD WRAP-UP

Congratulations! You've created a depression environment that proliferates negative thoughts and shields you from hope—a kind of bomb shelter with the bombs *in* it. This is a giant leap. Defeating happiness no longer means sadness. It means emptiness. A great big hole. That's right, not even sorrow wants to hang out with you anymore. Keep up those depressed thoughts and, over time, you will feel more and more removed from the world around you.

Having second thoughts? Hang tight, there is sidesplitting fun and destruction headed your way. In the next chapter, you will feel inspired to make new, equally glum friends, while a closer examination of the happy will help you navigate the delightfully depressed road ahead.

YOU ARE NOT ALONE (BUT YOU *ARE* LONELY)

What if I told you everything you know about happy people is wrong? Until now, you probably believed happiness came from happy people. But, in fact, usually the opposite is true.

In fact, it's depressed folks who've been the major contributors to societal happiness and contentment. After all, progress and innovation are driven by misery and discontent. Behind the creation of every modern convenience is a depressed person yelling, "Christ! Why won't this work!" It's taken years of suffering and impatience to get to where we are today.

Fortunately, by the time you've read this chapter, you will no longer feel tempted by the empty candy-coated shell of the happy. Instead, you'll be inspired to assemble a community of your own. You might be asking, "Is that even possible? Who's sending an agenda and a phone list?" You'd be surprised. There are quite a few who enjoy being angry, resentful, and productive. The best part is, you don't have to get dressed up (or even shower) to see them.

WHAT YOU'RE WEARING IS FINE.

HAPPY PEOPLE ARE RUINING OUR LIVES

Happy people believe everything happens for a reason. They wake each morning (no snooze button) and forge on despite fires, earthquakes, and jury duty. They don't see smog, social injustice, or the damage of morning talk shows. Instead, they see roomy all-leather interiors, uncontaminated evidence, and witty conversation.

It is not surprising that most people remain unaware of the myths and misnomers that surround happy types. As a result, several unproven, unsubstantiated positive qualities have been linked to them. For example, most believe that the happy are inclined toward empathy. There are no statistics to support these claims. Happy people are always skipping forward while fixated on their goals. It's the depressed who really look around as they slog along. A great deal of depression is caused by taking on the suffering of others, having a strong sense of justice, and suffering the guilt and self-loathing that comes from undeserved privileges and comforts.

It's easy to confuse "happy" with "cheery," or an uplifting disposition. Keep in mind that there are different kinds of cheer. There's the cheer of simple congratulations (*Well done!* or *Way to go!*), and then there's something more sinister, like cheerleaders—a cheer that draws attention to oneself. That's what happy people do. Many assume the person with the kind, cheery disposition is happy. Wrong. More often, the person who smiles, makes a kind gesture, or says, "Is there anything more I can get for you?" is a depressed person disguising themselves as happy, just for you. As soon as they make you feel good, they go back to being miserable.

So forget everything you know about happy people. Without cheer, care, or the ability to innovate and advance, what are happy people good for? Whistling, creating prechoreographed dances, like the Electric Slide, and justifying our persistent annoyance. We're better than that.

HAPPINESS FOR SALE

Happy people see the world less clearly and ask that you do the same. Their big sales pitch is this: if you can just overlook facts, reality, and science, you could be happy, too! The following suggestions are from "experts" trying to sell you happy. Imagine people lying just to sell a book!

> "You can't have a plan for your day
> 'til you have a plan for your life."
> —Tony Robbins, *Unleash the Power Within*

Settle down, Tony. I'm just getting a coffee and doing some light housecleaning. Tony Robbins is genuinely uplifting. Think how happy you just got that you don't live with him.

> "Maybe truth and happiness
> antagonize each other."
> —Martin E. P. Seligman, *Learned Optimism*

That's because happiness is an idiot.
— Yours truly, Truth

> "You attract your dominant thoughts."
> —Rhonda Byrne, *The Secret*

Dominant? They're downright sadistic! They've got whips, chains, leather chaps, and a classified ad in BDSM weekly. And they torture me daily.

"First you believe, and then you see the Light.
Next, you go toward the Light.
Soon you are in the Light. Now you are the Light."
—Robert Holden, *Happiness Now!*

I Think I saw this in a documentary
about how moths die.

"If you believe it will work out,
you'll see opportunities. If you believe
it won't, you'll see obstacles."
—Dr. Wayne W. Dyer, *Staying on the Path*

If you believe in life after love, you'll enjoy Cher.

"If you want to prosper, you have
to learn to ignore reality."
—Jim Donovan, *Happy at Work*

You don't just have to ignore reality. You have to get your
credit card company, bank, and landlord to also ignore reality.
Try offering them Monopoly money, and then see if you can
ignore the reality of living on the streets.

"Man becomes what he thinks about."
—Morris E. Goodman, *The Secret* (movie)

If that were true, all men would be orgasms.
And women would be carbs.

URBAN MYTHS

Few have really seen happiness—or at least done more than glimpse it, but the lore looms so large that we are powerless to resist its pursuit. Throughout our lives, we'll return to those locations of confirmed happiness sightings, hoping for another quick brush. Perhaps, we'd be lucky enough to capture a blurry photo as evidence of our meeting with the ever-elusive "happy."

HAPPY MEALS

A two-for-one deal where one child swiftly loses a toy made oceans away by another child who never got to play with it in the first place. Happy Meals contain half the number of fries a growing youth needs to survive, and all the hormones of a cow in its prime. It's a way of saying, "I want to keep you alive, but I don't know for how long. Let's get started on these chemicals and see what you're made of."

HAPPY HOUR

Typically three hours, but never the right three. Health professionals say it is the beginning of the day that sets the tone, so why wait until the end to feel loose, relaxed, uninhibited? As things stand, Happy Hour begins before the workday's close and ends shortly thereafter, meaning most people have to leave work early to get some pleasure they can afford.

HAPPY HOLIDAYS!

Working adults have endured
commutes, bosses, and the
monthly terror of break-room
birthdays all for one purpose:
to escape those who raised them.
Yet each December, these same
adults conduct (long, arduous)
pilgrimages back to visit their
early captors—or, even worse,
their spouse's early captors. And,
in the cruelest of fates, one is
pressured to bring gifts to pacify
the new crop of loud, useless
minicaptives.

HAPPY BIRTHDAY

Remember how you felt the last
time you had to pull yourself off
the couch and buy a gift, write a
card, and spend cash to celebrate
a friend's birthday? Happy birthdays ended at age ten. True, the
excitement picked up again at age
twenty-one, but it was gone the
next morning and has not been
seen since.

HAPPILY EVER AFTER

Happily Ever After only happens
to those who survive spectacular
childhood tragedies. Unless you've
been locked in a tower, assaulted
by a wolf, or blighted by a witch's
curse, you don't stand a chance.

HAPPY ENDINGS

Whether the type that is cinematic
or the type you hope is not being
filmed, they all have the same
conclusion: you drifting off,
feeling slightly ashamed, and
dreaming of a life that is not yours.

BUILDING YOUR DEPRESSED COMMUNITY

Sharing time with depressed friends—whether they are obsessed, talkative, or angry—can be quite a catharsis. These friends will perform the important role of validating your experience without validating you. Often, the depressed friend sitting across from you must interrupt your valid thoughts with their more valid thoughts. Frustrating, but totally worth it! That's because these friendships will be among your most entertaining ones. The depressed have few pretentions. She cannot help but say what is on her mind. And when nothing is sacred, everything is hilarious.

Perhaps more important than what the depressed community will do for you is what they will not do for you. They will not tell you to cheer up; they will not reassure you that everything is going to work out; and most importantly, they will not try to sell you anything. It is so wonderful—almost as good as being alone.

WHAT TO LOOK FOR
Before you begin your search, it's important to clarify one element: depressing individuals are not the same as depressed people. Take your family for instance. Lots of depressing people there—just to be in the same room with them requires mind-altering drugs, alcohol, or security glass. However, as we've seen, those who cause depression are not necessarily depressed themselves.

WHERE TO LOOK

So where to find your depressed brethren? The obvious place to begin is your office. Some professions are chock-full of depressed people. This is especially true of the medical community. Doctors, dentists, and psychotherapists are among the most depressed.

Next, try the neighbors. The ones who venture out once a month in a robe and mismatched socks, with their recycling, are operating at about your speed.

Outside of these areas, try writing workshops or political-action campaigns. Other hotspots include discussion groups, angry book clubs, Green Party rallies, and the green rooms of comedy clubs.

WHERE NOT TO LOOK

Depressed people don't want to DIY it, or "make their own." If you find yourself in a neighborhood littered with "decorate your own cake," "make your own pizza," or "paint your own pottery" shops, get out quickly. A depressed person will not be there. The exception is a parent who is accompanying a child to one of these places. That parent is definitely depressed and in need of a friend.

WHAT TO DO WITH YOUR DEPRESSED FRIENDS

First, have them sign your guest book. This will be difficult. Depressed friends tend to be a tricky, nonconforming lot. Though they acknowledge the futility of everything, the depressed still don't want their information collected. Try calling your guest book something else, such as Registry of Complaints, Insults, and Injuries. The downside of this tactic is that each of your depressed friends will need several volumes.

DEPRESSED-FRIEND GUEST BOOK

IDENTIFYING INFO

Date: _____ Name: _____

Is this really your name? ☐ Yes ☐ No

If not, who are you hiding from? ☐ The Feds ☐ Family ☐ This guest book

What meds are you on? _____

What meds would you like to be on? _____

What meds should your host be on? _____

EVENT PREP

Did you even want to go out? ☐ Yes ☐ No ☐ Don't know, don't care

Did you: ☐ Shower ☐ Iron your clothes ☐ Do the least amount possible

THE PLAN

What was the big plan for tonight?

☐ Dinner   ☐ Entertainment   ☐ Other

☐ Coffee   ☐ Crime   ☐ There was never a plan

How did you feel about tonight's activity?

☐ Looking forward to it   ☐ Was hoping it'd be cancelled due

☐ Would like to forget about it   to illness, national emergency,
                                     or alien invasion

Reasons for socializing:

☐ Guilt   ☐ I've run out of interested listeners

☐ Racking up community service hours ☐ Anticipating foul play

☐ Hoping for free food/drinks   ☐ Hoping to cross paths with tall,

☐ Hoping to pull off diamond heist   dark stranger to take me away
   and enter a world of crime   from this hell

HOW DID IT GO?

A. Conversation

Depressing topics discussed:

- ☐ Death
- ☐ Economy
- ☐ Kids
- ☐ Religion
- ☐ Politics
- ☐ Alternate universes
- ☐ String theory
- ☐ Sports
- ☐ Did Oswald act alone?
- ☐ News
- ☐ People judged
- ☐ Scenarios of doom
- ☐ The frosted side/ the wheat side
- ☐ _____

Did you:
- ☐ Learn something new
- ☐ Reveal a secret you'll later regret
- ☐ Stop paying attention halfway through

Over the course of the conversation, did you tell any lies? ☐ Yes ☐ No
How many? _____ How many times do you believe you were lied to? _____

B. Money

Was money spent, gambled, or lost? ☐ Yes ☐ No
If so, how much? $_____

Do you feel the cost was evenly split among participants? ☐ Yes ☐ No

Do you feel ripped off? ☐ Yes ☐ No
Were you the one ripping others off? ☐ Yes ☐ No

C. Food

Reasons for eating:

- ☐ Hungry
- ☐ Underentertained
- ☐ Feeling undervalued
- ☐ Subduing low-level anxiety
- ☐ Because it was there
- ☐ _____

Were these plans worth leaving home for?
☐ Yes   ☐ No   ☐ Before I can give my final verdict,
              I need to see how the rest of my life works out

DEPRESSED-FRIEND ACTIVITIES

Look at each other's scars, go for a slow and resentful walk, play cards, meet at the coffee shop, and share stories pertaining to a chosen theme, like "scenes from my pathetic life."

Discuss news, politics, medical symptoms, and attention-stealing siblings. Soon, it will seem like second nature. Until then, here are more fun depressed activities to choose from.

PLAY SOLITAIRE

Just because you're together doesn't mean you can't *feel* alone. Do your own thing while sharing an uncomfortably small space. Depressed friends understand you have more important things to do (or not do) because they have even more important things to do (or not do).

COMPARE SSRIs & MORE!

Compare illnesses, ailments, and diagnosis. Include your medications and undesired side effects. Create a list of desired side effects. "Some patients report side effects like fireworks, the appearance of unicorns, backup dancers, and a laser-light-beam show."

GET A NEW SYNDROME

Pick up pamphlets with new syndromes invented by Big Pharma. Tingly Nail Syndrome, Sticky Toes Syndrome, and Stretchy Burning Knees are fun options to consider. Or, better yet, see if you can make up some of your own!

RECOUNT PARENTAL ERRORS
Compare mistakes made by each of your parents. During the bonus round, make a list of unique and spectacular errors you would each be willing to make with your own offspring. Have an impartial third party decide which list would result in the most riotously dysfunctional child.

PLAY WORST-POSSIBLE OUTCOME
Make long-term predictions and wagers for celebrities, politics, big news events, and each other. The best part about a gamble on Worst-Possible Outcome is that even if you win, you lose.

CURATE A SAD-ART EXHIBIT
See who can capture the most depressing face or scenario of the day. Extra points for "funny-sad."

DO MAGIC TRICKS
Go out to a public place. Close your eyes. Visualize idiots. Open your eyes. There they are!

MAKE YOUR OWN!

A simple way to build up a depressed posse is to raise your own. Creating depressed offspring is a challenge for even the most determined of parents. Sure, your folks made it look easy. But a mere unhappy childhood does not guarantee a depressed life. Depression is not as much the result of the sadness of your circumstances as your unique outlook on them. In many cases, a happy childhood is the best setup for a depressed life.

As a parent, the best you can do is hang sandbags of insecurity and doubt that will drop on your children at an opportune moment. Upon successful completion, you will have yourself an in-house depression posse! Here are some recommendations to get you started:

THE BEDTIME STORY
Allow your child to select a bedtime story. When you have finished the book, offer a full critique and deconstruction of the story, characters, and plot. Make sure your child gets the idea that openly and fully enjoying something only leads to a backlash.

STOKE RIVALRY
Allow only one of your children to call you Mom or Dad at any given time. Never disclose the rules of the game or why the favor changes.

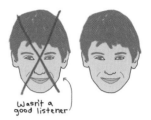

Wasn't a
good listener

MOVIES

By age five, make sure to screen
One Flew Over the Cuckoo's Nest
and *Girl, Interrupted* for your
child. Explain nothing. Just turn
up the volume and leave the room.

TWINS!

Convince your child he was a
twin, and tell him that while you
can't disclose the fate or where-
abouts of the other twin, suffice it
to say he wasn't a good listener.

CRUSH VOLUNTEERISM

When your child shows an interest in helping others, explain the
futility of her efforts. Explain
that one meal doesn't help the
homeless. Instead, diagram the
complex bureaucracy that stands
between them and progress.

GET DIVORCED

Get divorced. When your child
says, "But you're not divorcing
me, right? I'll still see you." Do
not respond. Simply hand her a
list of lawyers in the area.

NOT ALONE BUT LONELY WRAP-UP

You're now armed with information to see through the commercialism and resist the empty promises of the happy. You can now assemble a group, stand among your own kind, and feel totally alone. The knowledge that there is no comfort, or true catharsis, and that no one can understand you will hopefully enable you to enter a full-blown panic, just in time to fall into the arms of yet another fellow incompetent.

That's right, treatment is next. Get that checkbook ready for fifty fun minutes of useless understanding. Until then, sit back, tense up, and find a depressed friend to mock the next part of your journey—and every part thereafter.

TREATMENT (HOW TO MAKE IT NOT WORK FOR YOU)

Now that you are comfortably swaddled in your depression, it's a good time to get the professional validation that you are, in fact, a total whack job.

There are a number of reasons for doing this. First and foremost, you've got nothing better to do. In addition, avoiding life and responsibility requires a continuous flow of pharmaceuticals, diagnoses (yes, plural), and notes from mental-health professionals informing your boss that arriving before 2PM could threaten your delicate state.

Over the course of this chapter, you will receive an overview of the traditional treatment options available, as well as some of the more cutting-edge, lunatic ones. Regardless of which you choose, you will find an endless number of options on how to spend your family's money while whining about them.

HAPPY PILLS—YAY.

WHERE TO TURN:
THERAPIST, PSYCHIC, DOG?

No one is paying attention to (or cares about) your story—especially not the professionals. So, before you go in search of a trained therapist, it might be wise to consider alternate resources at your disposal.

Determine your priorities and use this chart to decide which type of assistance is appropriate for you.

	ADVANTAGES	DISADVANTAGES
THERAPIST	· No one else in session to refute your side of the story · Will never be told TMI · With a single sheet of letterhead, can convert your dog to a service animal	· Unable to solve your problems over drinks · You will have to answer the question "And how is that working out for you?" a total of 3,246 times · Does not lick your face
PSYCHIC	· May get a message from the dead · Available after 11PM · Can get a tattoo and funnel cake on the same trip	· Might switch tents without notifying you · Accepts cash only · Not an in-network service provider
DOG	· Nonjudgmental · Flexible scheduling · Will lick your face	· Have to feed it · Will make you feel like you're chasing your tail · Veterinarian costs more than an actual therapist

CHILD	· May not have a solution but will have Ritalin · Be the cautionary tale to youth you were meant to be · Will say anything for candy	· You may become the subject of show-and-tell · Will also find your boss baffling · Will call you a stupid-face and be right!
MOM	· Do the laundry while airing your dirty laundry · Bring blame directly to the source · Might get you cut from holiday festivities	· Guilt almost as hard to swallow as Mom's meatloaf · Risk being reminded she's cleaned up enough of your messes · Might get you cut from will
YOUR LOCAL BARISTA	· Is required to clean up whatever you spill · Couch available · No appointment necessary	· Have to shout your problems to be heard over the blender · Session might be disrupted by pretentious jerk who just wants coffee · Might be out crazied by loiterers
CLERGY	· Refreshments after service · Will put in a good word with God · You can experience that holier-than-thou feeling	· Might be asked to stay for the whole service · Expected to forgive thyself, and the church · Have to reconcile guilt of believing it's all bull while secretly hoping it works
GOD	· Cut out the middleman and go straight to the top! · Willing to travel · Won't interrupt (hopefully), but any reply confirms your need for professional help	· Advice won't hold up in court · Your voice may be hard to distinguish among all the others · Might feel pressured into buying his book

PSYCHOLOGIST, ANALYST, OR SOCIALIST?

FINDING THE THERAPIST THAT IS RIGHT FOR YOU

One of depression's greatest joys is sitting across from a professional head nodder who, for fifty minutes, will appear mildly interested while assembling a grocery list in his head.

The work of any legitimate therapist is to declare how grave your circumstances are while also highlighting how heroic and fragile your state is. It keeps her paid—and keeps you from having to create actual change. It makes you both feel better.

Every so often, a therapist (MSW, MFT, PsyD) will suggest how you could make a better choice. This is the perfect time to remind him who holds the sliding-scale checkbook. Offer a little "I might need to cancel next week," and you return to your role as the lead protagonist.

Pricing a therapist is like buying a car. She states an outrageous sum while trying not to burst out laughing. You respond with stunned silence during which you consider that even sex professionals work the entire hour (and bring condoms). Your first step toward wellness is staying quiet until your therapist says, "But I will work with you."

Negotiate a good deal for yourself and you'll have secured the perfect therapist—one you can complain about for years to come.

BUYER BEWARE

STATE LICENSE OR MONOGRAM?

Licensing varies from state to state (because they're making it up). It's up to you to be vigilant. Buyer beware, initials do not make a qualified provider. L.L.Bean puts initials on towels, so you can imagine how easy they are to add to signs, certificates, and diplomas.

WHAT YOU SHOULD SEEK:
MSW, Masters of Social Work
PsyD, Doctor of Psychology
PhD, Doctor of Philosophy

WHAT YOU MAY GET:		
Name	**Actual License**	**Tip-Off**
Ray P. Reilly, MSG	Monosodium Glutamate	Fun session but afterward, you will feel tired and bloated
Leonard Steel, PSD	Adobe Photoshop Data File, .psd	Asks if you want to update your software
Jodi Hershel, PSA	Public Service Announcement	Wears Just Say No T-shirt
Lee Young, PBS	Public Broadcasting Service	Closes each session by saying, "This session is made possible by patients like you."
Edward Altman, PHL	Philadelphia International Airport	Often cancels or is delayed due to "acts of God"

LESSER-KNOWN THERAPIES

Western medicine has been criticized for its narrow approach, especially by those who can't meet the demands of showing up, accepting responsibility, and facing the horror of change. "Eastern" medicine, however, is open to a wide range of techniques provided by nut jobs who screwed up their own lives and would now like a shot at yours.

At this point, there are so many types of therapy, it would be completely reasonable to seek a new solution every few weeks. In fact, you should consider an alternate approach anytime you feel you might be nearing actual change.

Check out some of the more creative and eccentric ways to begin transforming yourself from the outside in!

ART THERAPY

Express your emotions through sculpture, drawing, and paint. Like the work of the masters, everyone will take one look, gasp, and say, "I don't get it." You must be a genius.

SILENT THERAPY

Stare into the eyes of the therapist long enough to realize *Holy crap, this person is crazier than me!*

WINNING THERAPY

Let the games begin. Approach everything as if it were a competition. If you and a random stranger head toward the door, rush to open it first, grinning at their weakness. If your significant other wants to lose weight, lose more, faster. If your Nana gets sick, get sicker. Carry a notebook and record each day's major (and minor!) triumphs.

CROWD-FUNDING THERAPY

See how much people are willing to invest in order to fix you.

CRYING THERAPY

People fear tears. The idea that they caused someone to cry challenges their notion of self. To make up for it, they'll start handing over croissants or sick days. Work up some tears and you'll see the waters part.

CAR THERAPY

Within the safe confines of your car, scream at drivers who hesitate, forget to signal, or signal but don't move. As you shout, "Unbelievable!" and "Are you kidding me?" you release anger and confirm your long-held suspicion that even though you feel inadequate, you're far more competent than anyone else.

TYPES OF THERAPISTS

Just as there are multiple approaches to therapy, there are multiple types of therapists. The way a therapist responds to your endless jabber is not taught in schools. Rather, it reflects the therapist's inborn gifts. It's the same way that athletes possess different talents. Some are good at throwing the ball; others at kicking it. You are the therapist's ball. The way your therapist reacts to you indicates how well he has integrated your life and problems into his own.

THE ME-TOO THERAPIST
For almost everything you say, the Me-Too Therapist has had the very same thing happen to her! Perhaps she should be coming to *you* for therapy.

THE DISNEY THERAPIST
Having spent too much time at hand-holding retreats and campfires, the Disney Therapist appears to be shocked anytime you share a story of harsh or unkind treatment. This reaction gives you the sneaking suspicion she lives in that room all the time and is assisted by dwarfs, mice, or dalmatians.

THE UN-SELF-AWARE THERAPIST
This therapist has a facial tick, arm spasm, or tongue click that he never addresses. It makes you want to say, "Thank you for caring. Now what are we going to do about *your* problem?"

HEAVY-LIDS THERAPIST
Heavy Lids is straining, doing all he can to keep his eyes open for your boring life. Often, he'll blame allergies or contact lenses, but take the hint: he thinks you should be sleeping through your problems too.

GREY GARDENS THERAPIST

Grey Gardens Therapist lives in his office. He's obviously been in there many years as evidenced by the piles of books, files, and old lunches that fill the room. Before getting treatment, have a sharp look around to make sure he's *treating* hoarders and not just storing them in his closet.

THE TELL-IT-LIKE-IT-IS THERAPIST

Someone's been watching too much *Dr. Phil* and, upon hearing of your misfortune, will want to point out all of the red flags you missed. Simply explain you have no ability to detect disaster. If you did, you wouldn't be in his office.

VALIDATING THERAPIST

The Validating Therapist is there to comfort you. She backs up everything you say with, "Wow, that must have been difficult for you." Well, not as difficult as all this pandering.

FEAR OF ABANDONMENT THERAPIST

Fear of Abandonment will always lift you up when you're down. But should your improved state lead to notions of independence and a therapy-free life, FOA will be the first to remind you what a basket case you are.

SIDE-EFFECTS WORD SCRAMBLE

(COMMON SIDE EFFECTS OF
YOUR SEROTONIN REUPTAKE INHIBITOR)

1. LUERDBR IIOVSN
2. XALSUE STYNFNICODU
3. NICTAOOPNTSI
4. NOFSCONUI
5. ENSESNOUVSR
6. TGWHEI INAG
7. AHIR OSLS
8. RDY MUHOT
9. LNIITGGN TFEE
10. ESEPL EDBCRSANSIUT
11. ONGMIVTI
12. IEVXSESEC AESWTING
13. NGNAIYW
14. LUNRTCBAOOLLNE AKIGHSN
15. HETAR UBRN
16. SRZESUIE
17. NUYRN OSEN
18. UHISGFNL
19. CUMLES ENWSSKAE
20. ISTNIEIVYTS OT ILHGT
21. EENIGFL REDDUGG
22. APNI NI AKCB UELCMSS TOSJNI RO ENARWYEH NI HET ODBY

ANSWERS: 1. blurred vision 2. sexual dysfunction 3. constipation 4. confusion 5. nervousness 6. weight gain 7. hair loss 8. dry mouth 9. tingling feet 10. sleep disturbances 11. vomiting 12. excessive sweating 13. yawning 14. uncontrollable shaking 15. heart burn 16. seizures 17. runny nose 18. flushing 19. muscle weakness 20. sensitivity to light 21. feeling drugged 22. pain in back, muscles, joints, or anywhere in the body

PSYCHIATRIC EVALUATION:
A Doom of Her Own

PATIENT INFORMATION

Patient Name: Adeline Virginia Woolf

Lived: Jan 25, 1882 - March 28, 1941

Employment: Determination

Career Highlights:
- Featured on the stamp of Romania
- Sculpture of bust in Tavistock Square, London
- 2014 tribute exhibition at the national Portrait museum

Career Lowlights:
Being dead for all the highlights

CASE HISTORY

Risk Factors:
- Overcast skies of Kensington and pretty much anywhere she went.
- Unmanageable hair.
- No access to wite-out
- Her motherland's undying allegiance to cricket.
- Wrote To the Lighthouse, but didn't get to go to the lighthouse.

Personal and Social History:
Born to a blended family at a time when blended families were not yet the subject of psychological study and television situation comedies, an era known as B.J.B. (Before Jan Brady).

Education:
Virginia was homeschooled by her mother, a former model who stood for many painters. It is believed that at the end of the school day, the beautiful but aged Mrs. Stephen would line up her children and announce: "I have five children, but only four photos in my hand. The person who is not called must pack her bags immediately..."

Psycho-Social Development:
Was surrounded by death from an early age (and not the funny kind). Her mother passed when she was thirteen years old, followed by the death of her half-sister, which was half-heartbreaking. Luckily they didn't have pets.

Recommended Treatment:
- Have a room of your own but open the bed to visitors.
- Water wings!
- Don't be British. However, if you must be, invest in a full-spectrum lamp or tanning bed.
- For teatime, switch to decaf.
- Don't hang out with writers.

THINGS YOU SHOULDN'T SAY TO YOUR THERAPIST

What research is this advice based on?

I see dead people.

What would I have to do to be committed?

Seriously, where's the certificate?

Maybe you should work with animals because they can't understand you either.

How can we get everyone around me to change instead?

If you were following me on Twitter you'd know how my week was!

I love you.

I bet I can make you cry.

Can I get your home address?

I brought a bottle of pinot, so we could relax and get to know one another.

Yes, Alex, I'll take Bad Childhood for $500!

Do you want to observe me in my natural environment?

Can I get a note on letterhead telling everyone that I'm right?

Manic? I'm not manic. You think I'm manic!
THAT'S CRAZY!

THINGS YOU HOPE YOUR THERAPIST DOESN'T SAY TO YOU

Have you thought about pills?

These are my regular rates, but I'm going
to have to charge you more.

I'm listening—I just need to close my eyes.

According to your horoscope...

I have a wonderful time-share you might be interested in.

Do you mind if I film this?

I'm feeling insecure today. Do you find me attractive?

Do you want to read my screenplay?
It's based on our work together.

Have you thought about Scientology? I have an in.

You were in my dream last night.

Oh, you're my 2 o'clock appointment! That's so weird,
you look just like my 5 o'clock. Okay, start again.

Your problem reminds me of the
Israeli-Palestinian conflict, but less solvable.

My cousin's getting married in June and I don't have a date.
Want to be my plus-one? Chicken or fish?

I know a great psychic.

TREATMENT WRAP-UP

Well, that's all the time we have. Did you bring a check? Over the course of the past fifty minutes, you've been exposed to some pretty unsubstantiated research for treating the mind. It should be more clear than ever that you are beyond help. The best you can hope for in your pursuit of treatment is a good laugh. Otherwise, anyone offering you help in all likelihood needs it more than you.

Here is the big takeaway: as New Age–treatment techniques have broadened the definition of therapy, you have the option of selecting any activity and calling it therapy. You can buy a bearded dragon lizard, dress it in a vest, and claim it's an emotional support animal. Guess who never has to go to the movies alone again?

The next (and final!) chapter will supply you with a grab bag of fun, random activities—games, puzzles, jokes—for those rare days when you can muster enough energy to pretend you are not actually depressed at all.

FUN WITH DEPRESSION!

You probably didn't know this, but depression loves fun. It especially loves jokes. That's why it puts so much sarcasm and judgment into your head. As you'll see in this chapter, you and depression can have heaps of fun with jokes, activities, games, puzzles, and even some light shopping.

Here's the best part. Only you get to have fun with your depression. No one else. You can make all the jokes you'd like. If a happy friend (aka "a Normal") cracks a joke about depression, meds, or mental health, you should immediately inform them how offended you are by their lack of sensitivity. If a Normal is being encouraging and empathetic, shout, "Heard it! Doesn't help!"

Depression is a fun-loving companion because it gives you permission to do anything in the name of feeling good. Don't worry about having too much fun or feeling too good. Not a chance.

YOU'LL LAUGH SO HARD YOU'LL CRY (EVEN MORE).

FINDING YOUR DEPRESSION ALIAS

You need a name that captures the essence of your sad, pathetic self. Find your depression alias by selecting the most shameful quality of your home and combining it with your worst physical attribute. This is a scientifically proven method to yield your most fitting Depression alias.

FILL IN YOUR DEPRESSION ALIAS:

_____

_____

STEP 1	STEP 2
Declare the Most Shameful Aspect of Your Home	**Add Your Worst Physical Attribute**
1. Greasy	1. Big Nose
2. Musty	2. Freckles
3. Dusty	3. Cankles
4. Messy	4. Man Boobs (aka "Moobs")
5. Peeling	5. Wide Thighs
6. Stained	6. Stringy Hair
7. Moldy	7. Muffin Top
8. Leaky	8. Thin Lips
9. Drippy	9. Pig Nose
10. Rusty	10. Unibrow
11. Cracked	11. Uniboob
12. Dim	12. Front Butt
13. Sticky	13. Buckteeth
14. Smelly	14. Jowls
15. Crumby	15. Third Nipple
16. Filthy	16. Potbelly
17. Dumpy	17. Frizzy Hair
18. Drafty	18. Gummy Smile
19. Damp	19. Giant Pores
20. Scuzzy	20. Skinny Legs
21. Creaky	21. Bulging Eyes
22. Bleak	22. Distracting Mole
23. Crumbly	23. Back Fat
24. Mossy	24. Short Arms
25. Damaged	25. No Neck

BONUS ROUND—MAKE IT VIRAL!

For extra fun and five seconds of potential internet fame, add the last two
digits of your birth year to your new name and stick a hashtag on it!

#MustyCankles84   #FilthyThirdNipple91   #StickyJowls69

13 BOOKS to CHEER YOU UP!
(Because 10 is not enough)

1. The Noonday Demon: An Atlas of Depression by Andrew Solomon

2. The Bell Jar by Sylvia Plath

3. One hundred Years of Solitude by Gabriel García Márquez

4. Vegan Cooking for One by Leah Leneman

5. Eat, Pray, Love by Elizabeth Gilbert (Because no publisher will ever foot the bill for your trip.)

6. Catcher in the Rye, Night, Of mice and Men, Lord of the Flies (or all other High school books you didn't realize were preparing you for life.)

7. Sleisenger and Fordtran's Gastrointestinal and Liver Disease 2 Volume Set: Pathophysiology, Diagnosis, Management (10th Edition) by Mark Feldman, MD; Lawrence S. Friedman MD; and Lawrence J. Brandt, MD

8. The Handmaid's Tale by Margaret Atwood

9. How to Save Your Marriage Alone by Ed Wheat, MD

10. Diving Bell & The Butterfly by Jean-Dominique Bauby (Because he gets to stay in bed.)

11. The Giving Tree by Shel Silverstein

12. War and Peace by Leo Tolstoy (or anything classified under Russian Literature.)

13. How to Be Depressed: A Guide by Dana Eagle

DEPRESSING PETS

A pet embodies your attitude toward outsiders. It can growl, bite, destroy, or take a dump on the neighbor's lawn. As the beast's owner, you get to create excuses for behavior that conveniently expresses your own frustrations. He has anxiety. He's feeling unloved. He feels broke and unappreciated. He needs a new iPhone. He doesn't like Steelers fans.

And, just like your pet, you are an indiscriminate eater, willing to wolf down a found piece of food from the floor just to fill the empty spaces. (But unlike your pet, you didn't even do a smell check first.)

And perhaps the characteristic you and your pet most have in common is your ability to completely turn your back on others once you've gotten what you need.

We are a lot alike.

CONSIDER THE KITTY

A cat is a can't miss for the depressed. With a cat by your side (or under the bed), it is no longer necessary to announce that you are depressed. The cat hair stuck to your clothes is a dead giveaway of how little you care.

Every aspect of caring for a cat is inherently sad, like buying meager cans of food that you will stack chin high, both for economy and for grocery-store humiliation. Then there is kitty cleanup: the litter, sticky bowls, and astonishing amounts of vomit and hair balls.

Unlike dogs, cats don't take slippers or newspapers. They go for the larger pieces that are replaced every decade or so, like the sofa or the wall-to-wall carpeting. After a while, you acclimate to life in fabric-torn territories. It's like depression pregaming.

Cat urine is another plus. You will no doubt fall for every infomercial, offer, or natural bottle spray that claims it can remove the smell of cat urine. Nothing can remove the smell of cat urine.

Not convinced that the domesticated cat is the right depressed animal for you? Step out gently, and support a family of feral furries. These are creatures who don't live in your home but lurk around it. Feed them once, and you'll be the loved leader of the free cat nation. (By the way, they're all free. Shelters, homes, Craigslist can't give them away quickly enough.) You will feel purposeful, revered, a custodian of god's creatures. But really, they just want the food.

KITTY FEATURES AND UPGRADES

- Must be kept in multiples
- Should be hairless, Not because of the breed but because of some sort of nervous condition or allergy that causes patchiness, hair loss, and skin flaking.
- Ideally suffers from acid reflux. (Luckily for you, they all do.)

CONSIDER THE CANINE

With proper selection and ambivalent care, a dog will walk your depression in a circle and send you back where you started. In fact, several times a day, you'll walk around the same loop, pull pup's head away from the same tree, and interact with the same neighbors, most of whom employ their dog as a fitness trainer. That's right, you have a membership to the cheapest, most static gym ever. Not only are walks and commands repetitive, they'll also force you to cycle through the same five topics of conversation (four of which will be about the dog).

Unless you picked up your pooch from a doggie senior center, it might take a little time for you both to get in step with depression. Stick with it. A dog might enter your home with enthusiasm, but before long she'll pick up on your cues of fatigue and exasperation.

In order to speed up the slow-down process, buy a purebred. The only thing sadder than a rescue with the anxiety and jumpiness of a Vietnam War veteran is a gorgeous, dumb purebred whose back leg lags due to generations of inbreeding. You'll have daily amusement followed by guilt when you hear her picturesque head hit the side of the door frame because the vision in her left eye is fading. Watch those vet bills pile up. She's like a Jaguar—impressive and fun for the three hours a year she's not in the shop.

Yes, a dog will be a bit more of a hill to climb to reach your depression apex, but between traumatized rescues and demented purebreds, you'll find the one that will slouch by your side. But only because you have it on a leash. Otherwise, it'd rather go back and eat the puke you walked by. Now give Mommy kisses!

CANINE FEATURES AND UPGRADES

- Think fearful and neurotic. Choose a dog that's scared of birds, flies, and the remote control.
- Get a leaky dog: leaky mouth, leaky eyes, and yikes, you're gonna need deluxe size wee pads.
- Ideally suffers from a pastiche of chronic and inexplicable symptoms that results in mobility issues. Pick a fur baby that looks like a show dog but digs through trash like a street rat. Dumpster diving could prove useful someday.

OFF THE BEATEN PET PATH

None of these depressed companions would be described as man's best friend or precocious, but each has a compelling reason to be a part of your depressed setting.

THE IGUANA
Will show you the same amount of affection that your ex did.

THE HERMIT CRAB
You get to decide when it's dead.

SIAMESE FIGHTING FISH
Like you, it cannot live among its own kind, and it manages to be unusual and boring at the same time. Bonus: It lives in its own urine.

ANY FISH
Once flushed, you get to display the empty bowl as a reminder life has left your home.

FRUIT FLIES
Whether you want them or not, you *will* have fruit fly pets.

DEPRESSION INACTION FIGURES
COLLECT THE WHOLE SET!

This season give your children (or your sad self) the gift of InAction Figures: dolls and figurines so wrapped up in themselves, they don't even have time to play. Experts agree this new lineup of afflicted and unstable pals is the perfect tool for teaching children how disappointing everyone can be.

Order InAction Figures now, and start your child on the path of inappropriate shares, soul-sucking relationships, hysteria, and helplessness.

POSTPARTUM POLLY

LOW SELF-ESTEEM LARRY

COMES WITH:
Screaming baby, bottle of vodka, birth control, useless husband, and a photo album (of her wonderful life before children).

PULL POLLY'S STRING AND SHE SAYS:
"Now I know why they say don't drink during pregnancy. You're going to need to drink after."

COMES WITH:
Catalog of Learning Annex seminars, stack of tiny self-help books (e.g., *I'm Okay—You're Probably Better*), and list of mantras, such as "I like myself! (even though no one else does)."

PULL LARRY'S STRING AND HE SAYS:
"Dreams <u>do</u> come true. For everyone else."

BIPOLAR BELINDA

AGORAPHOBIC AL

COMES WITH:
Untouched lithium (because she's much better now!), luxury yacht purchased on a whim, and a sixty-page bucket list that begins with "Live among the Aborigines" and ends with "Nap."

PULL BELINDA'S STRING AND SHE SAYS:
"This is horrible! Half the time."

COMES WITH:
Hermetically sealed airtight house, order-in menus, and bulletin board of clippings showcasing tragic accidents, like "Man trips and falls to his death" and "Squirrel attacked by pigeons."

PULL AL'S STRING AND HE SAYS:
"I'm not home!"

S.A.D.
(SEASONAL AFFECTIVE DISORDERED)
STEVEN

O.C.D. CARRIE

COMES WITH:
Farmer's Almanac, map of Seattle, T-shirt, and a full-spectrum light smashed into 200 pieces.

PULL STEVEN'S STRING AND HE SAYS:
"The countdown to Daylight savings."

COMES WITH:
Hospital mask, purse containing hand sanitizer, sanitizer primer, and sanitizer sealant, and hair-dryer with note stuck to it that says, "Did you unplug this?"

PULL CARRIE'S STRING AND SHE SAYS:
"If only I could remember what I'm forgetting."

LOSER LOLLY

HYPOCHONDRIAC HARRY

COMES WITH:
Pile of rejection letters, trophy labeled "Perfect Attendance Record," and imaginary friends who are too busy to play.

PULL LOLLY'S STRING AND SHE SAYS:
"You don't know what you're not capable of until you try..."

COMES WITH:
Physicians Desk Reference, blood-sugar monitor, calendar of daily doctor appointments, mobility scooter, and an Explanation of Benefits letter from Blue Cross.

PULL HARRY'S STRING AND HE SAYS:
"Look at this rash. Definitely cancer."

13 FLICKS TO CHEER YOU UP!
(Because 10 is not enough)

1. Precious
2. Love Story
3. Leaving Las Vegas
4. 1980s After-School specials starring Scott Baio warning about drugs
5. My Life as a Dog
6. Schindler's List or anything genocide-y
7. Dancer in the Dark
8. 12 Years a Slave
9. Requiem for a Dream
10. Sybil
11. Million Dollar Baby (or anything with Hilary Swank)
12. Boyhood
13. The Elephant Man

Author's Note: Use caution with any film depicting slavery, the holocaust, genocide, or gay/transgender hate. It may make you feel like you have no right to be depressed. And you do.

WHAT'S WRONG WITH ME?
MOODY CATCHER

Seek the reliable services of a fifth-grade fortune teller. Before you were broken, it was there to tell your favorite color, your favorite number, and which classmate to kiss. Now it will narrow things down to a few simple elements beyond your control. It may not have all the answers but it certainly asks the crucial question.

MOODY CATCHER INSTRUCTIONS

FUN DEPRESSING FOODS

You can eat anything (and everything!) while you're depressed, but the advantage of the following foods is that they're already depressing, whether you're there or not.

EGG SALAD

OATMEAL

FISH SANDWICH
from burger joint

MEATLOAF

JELL-O
with pineapple bits

SARDINES

ANY SINGLE-SERVING FOOD
PACKAGED FOR PORTION CONTROL,
EVEN THOUGH IT'S A FOOD PURCHASED
SOLELY FOR THE PURPOSE OF PIGGING OUT

DAY-OLD FRUIT
SALAD SOURED
BY ORANGE SLICES

GAS STATION
SANDWICH OR
SALAD

SCONES
(or anything prepared by
the British)

CANNED MEAL-REPLACEMENT
SHAKES THAT CLAIM TO
KEEP YOU FULL ALL DAY

CHICKENLESS CHICKEN,
MEATLESS MEATBALLS, OR
SOY HOT DOGS

ANYTHING
WITH RAISINS

DEPRESSION

ARIES

ZODIAC SYMBOL

DEPRESSION SYMBOL

THE RAM

MEDICAL HELMET

CANCER

ZODIAC SYMBOL

DEPRESSION SYMBOL

THE CRAB

TISSUE BOX

TAURUS

ZODIAC SYMBOL

DEPRESSION SYMBOL

THE BULL

STRAITJACKET

LEO

ZODIAC SYMBOL

DEPRESSION SYMBOL

THE LION

RESTRAINING ORDER

GEMINI

ZODIAC SYMBOL

DEPRESSION SYMBOL

THE TWINS

TWO PILES OF PILLS

VIRGO

ZODIAC SYMBOL

DEPRESSION SYMBOL

THE MAIDEN

LOBOTOMY

HORRORSCOPES

LIBRA

ZODIAC SYMBOL

DEPRESSION SYMBOL

THE SCALES

TRUTH SERUM

CAPRICORN

ZODIAC SYMBOL

DEPRESSION SYMBOL

THE GOAT

BARF BAG

SCORPIO

ZODIAC SYMBOL

DEPRESSION SYMBOL

THE SCORPION

SYRINGE

AQUARIUS

ZODIAC SYMBOL

DEPRESSION SYMBOL

RITALIN

THE WATER BEARER

RITALIN

SAGITTARIUS

ZODIAC SYMBOL

DEPRESSION SYMBOL

BALL GAG

THE ARCHER

PISCES

ZODIAC SYMBOL

DEPRESSION SYMBOL

THE FISH

FISH FLOATING IN THE TOILET BOWL

DEPRESSION HORRORSCOPES

ARIES

Your drive to get ahead brings you flashy clothes and material goods. They're nice to stare at while you wonder why all your loved ones always leave you.

TAURUS

Once you make the decision to be depressed you stick with it. When you're going through hell, you keep going. Even if it means plodding past clearly marked exit ramps.

GEMINI

You'll try anything to communicate your needs, including writing, screaming, and taking out ads. Maybe one day you'll try listening.

CANCER

You always see the tissue box as half empty, but it's actually completely empty. Use your sensitive nature to perceive any possible slight, no matter how tiny or far-fetched.

LEO

You turn your magnificent pride into a surprising depression advantage as you wonder, again and again, why no one appreciates you or notices your critical contributions to everything.

VIRGO

As effective as you are at bumming out others, your depression really catches fire when you turn that perfectionistic nature on yourself. Dig in and don't cut yourself a single break.

LIBRA
Your propensity to weigh and measure all your options is the perfect reason to never actually go anywhere or get anything done. Or should you? Maybe now? Or later? Probably later.

SCORPIO
Your deep, dark, passionate nature lets you take brooding to a level most people only encounter in German expressionism marathons.

SAGITTARIUS
There is a tree in the woods. It fell. Did you hear it? 'Cause it said you wouldn't shut the hell up!

CAPRICORN
When you're not busy with depression, you worry about failure. Which makes you more depressed. That's right, just like you, your depression just keeps going and going and going...

AQUARIUS
You have so many personalities to explore: depression plain, depression with a hat, depression with a cape, depression in a houndstooth blazer and pipe. Exhausting, isn't it?

PISCES
You swim in everyone else's depression waters. Seek support— again. You'll know when to cry when you see the others cry.

YOUR BAD POETRY

As an official member of the depressed masses, you're required to compose bad poetry. Below is a guide to take you through the steps of the first of many awful creations to come.

LINE 1
a) Dancing feet
b) Bright smiles
c) Dewy kittens
d) Shiny thoughts
e) Joyous butterflies
f) Compassion and understanding

LINE 2
a) decomposed
b) been trampled by elephants
c) been disqualified for placing bets on their own game
d) suffered a mafia hit
e) been charged with insider trading
f) suffered a disfiguring fireworks accident

LINE 3
a) truly see
b) know their torment
c) hear their screams
d) sense their darkness
e) feel the craving for Parmesan
f) taste their ennui

LINE 4
a) vision
b) comprehension
c) deep knowledge
d) empathy
e) paranoia
f) cojones

LINE 5
a) childhood
b) high school
c) college
d) grad school
e) book club
f) that weird parachute we played with in gym class on rainy days

LINE 6
a) angst
b) screams
c) darkness
d) puckered extremities
e) tingly scalp
f) weird rash behind my ear

LINE 7
a) deep enough
b) smart enough
c) aware enough
d) patient enough
e) self-absorbed enough
f) drunk enough

LINE 8
a) appreciate my complexity
b) shed a tear for my pain
c) buy me a drink
d) connect me with a wealthy benefactor
e) embrace my bizarre behavior as genius
f) make me their muse

LINE 1

_____

LINE 2

Have _____.

LINE 3

Only I _____.

LINE 4

Only I have the _____.

LINE 5

This is just like _____.

LINE 6

O, feel my _____.

LINE 7

If only other people were _____

LINE 8

To _____.

13 SONGS TO CHEER YOU UP!
(Because 10 is not enough)

1. "Landslide" (Stevie Nicks)
2. "Candle in the Wind" (Elton John)
3. "Gloomy Sunday" (Billie Holiday)
4. "Chasing Cars" (Snow Patrol), "Catalyst" (Anna Nalick), "How to Save a Life" (The Fray), or any other rock ballad made famous by a Grey's Anatomy death/scene.
5. "Seventeen" (Janis Ian)
6. "Fire and Rain" (James Taylor)
7. Anything by the Carpenters, Amy Winehouse, Sam Smith, or Adele.
8. "Hallelujah" (Jeff Buckley)
9. "Tears in Heaven" (Eric Clapton)
10. "Killing Me Softly" (Roberta Flack)
11. "Have Yourself a Merry Little Christmas" (Judy Garland), but only from November 1st to January 2nd. All other times of year, it's harmless.
12. Anything by Ashlee Simpson, Hilary Duff, David Hasselhoff, or Lindsay Lohan because they still had a better career than you.
13. If divorced, your wedding song.

4pm OPTIONS

COFFEE BREAK

DANCE BREAK

PSYCHOTIC BREAK

FUN WITH DEPRESSION WRAP-UP

Hey, there, depression champ! You've learned your depression can be entertaining! And not just for your therapist. You can partake in simple mindless activities while maintaining your melancholy roots.

As you move ahead, continue to explore not just the depression landscape but the unique facets of your own illness. Don't allow your depression to be put in a box, to be stereotyped into a formulaic *Silver Linings Playbook*, *Death of a Salesman*, or *Girl, Interrupted* caricature. At every turn, add elements to your depression to throw people off your trail and keep medical professionals on their toes.

Regardless of how your life story unfolds or the type of depressive you choose to become, don't lose sight of the fact that you can be fatigued and uncomfortable anywhere. So why not make the most of it? Continue to write your poetry, create your soundtrack, rehearse your breakdowns, and nurture your depression animal—both the inner and the outer.

And don't forget to take advantage of your privilege. As an esteemed member of the club, you are permitted to disrespect, taunt, and make fun of depression's hair. In fact, it's required. Sanctimony, piousness, and reverence are prohibited, and if witnessed acting out in such a way, you may be asked to go find yourself a different disease. Such behavior is not something to be taken lightly.

For now, though, continue to follow your path. There may be times during this journey when you feel like you are getting nowhere, that you're staying in one place. Learn to trust the heartache. You are coming along quite nicely. And for now, you have everything you need.

Wow! You thought this day would never come. Well, here it is! Not such a big deal after all. Nothing is.

You should know that by now.

DEPRESSION EPILOGUE

You've come to the end, so go, push away from the light . . . Find a mirror. Hold up the mirror. Stare. Yup, that's what a depressed person looks like. Who would've known? Other than every fiber of your being.

Right now, you may be wishing you had selected *How to Be Paranoid*, or *How to Be Obsessive-Compulsive*, or *How to Stop Purchasing How-To Books.*

Luckily for you, depression will complement whatever disease, disorders, or disasters your stormy heart desires. It is the white wine of ailments. It pairs well with anything, so feel free to mix and match.

Besides, you're good at this. You jumped right in there. Wow! Impressive! It's almost hard to believe this was your first time. Or was it?

You've now had the opportunity to perfect your technique and discover depression's greater purpose. Yes, your misery has purpose outside of Big Pharma, PajamaGrams, and TED Talks. It is from misery that you come to know humanity, gaining an appreciation and empathy for the outsider. And as an outcast, you've freed yourself from the constructs of happiness you were once fully indoctrinated into.

These are incredible strides. One might venture to say you possess all of the ingredients for happiness. Don't get ahead of yourself. What you possess, in fact, is the best companion depression could ask for. Humor. This will take you (and your depression) far. That is your gift. And there's no receipt.

HEY!
NICE SWEATPANTS.

ACKNOWLEDGMENTS

Gratitude and the finest champagne for my agent, Danielle Svectov, who led the way through this dynamic adventure.

Thank you and straight-up hard liquor for my editor, Erin Conley, who picked my project from her haystack, then patiently guided me, always letting me know when I made her laugh.

A round of shots for my wonderfully gifted and supportive friends Randi Barnes, John Bland, Jimmy Brogan, Rachel Brookhart, James P. Connolly, Ali Davis, Lisa Dickey, Kathleen Dennehy, Lee Levine, Cari Lynn, Ann Masters, Marc Mealie, Guy Nicolucci, Amy Scribner, Christian Skelly, Beth Sherman, Sascha Rothchild, Sam Shaber, George Strayton, and (the latest additions) Jean Bush, Paul Guerin, and Daniel Kurtzman.

For my manager, Justin Silvera, a primo double espresso because I don't think you'll get to sleep any time soon. Mostly though, because I know it's what you want and anything stronger is illegal.

A mai tai for my tireless lawyer, David J. Cohen, but more importantly, the beach that comes with it.

To the Shrinky Dinks: Those who came before, and to L. H., the remarkable one who gently nudged me into the now. An organic tea—because I hope that's all you're drinking during our sessions.

To the Druckers, Zaziks, and my own personal, loving, cuckoo's nest (Mom, Dad, and Scott): a glass of Manischewitz and a nosh for your ceaseless love, support, and sarcasm. (And because you're going to change the order anyway.)

This book is dedicated to the stand-up comedians, who'll have whatever the club is comping.

Thank you.

ABOUT THE AUTHOR

Dana Eagle grew up in New Jersey. She was her fifth-grade class president and has the distinction of surviving two impeachments and an assassination attempt. (She was later overthrown by a coup). She's made numerous TV appearances, including Comedy Central, *Last Comic Standing*, *The Tonight Show*, *The Late, Late Show*, and *Comics Unleashed*. Among her greatest memories are her trips to Iraq to perform for the troops. Dana's one-woman show was featured at the HBO US Comedy Arts Festival. She would like to be your spirit animal.